Installing Linux On PCs and Laptops

R. S. AKE

Installing Linux On PCs and Laptops
Copyright © 2024 by Robert Scott Ake

CONTENTS

INTRODUCTION

Linux places control and access in the hands of the users where it belongs. This book should be considered to be a set of working examples and recommendations. Your system, your rules.

"Installing Linux On PCs and Laptops", ILOPAL, is written for PC and Laptop users interested in installing Linux. This book focuses on installing Debian using Live install chips.

Installing Debian does not have to be a brutal all or nothing procedure. It can be a methodical process done in steps, and in fact, does not ever have to be installed on the system's hard drive/SSD. There is no need to be without a functioning system during the process.

The first step is to create a Debian Live USB stick. These chips are designed to work with Intel/AMD based PCs and Laptops. The next step is to change the boot order to boot from USB first. If needed, do an internet search on the **<manufacture>**, <model>, and **boot order**.

While booting most PCs and Laptops will have an option to select the **Boot Menu** or **Settings Menu**. The Boot Menu should allow manual selection of the boot device without making any permanent changes. The Settings Menu should allow the boot order to be permanently changed. Always take a picture of the boot order before making a permanent change (most cell phones have cameras). Some computers may have an option to return to factory settings.

Once a Debian Live USB stick has booted, Debian can be installed on an SD Card connected by a USB to SD card adapter. Issues with Debian can be resolved without affecting an existing OS on the hard drive/SSD. 128 GB is a good size for an SD card.

Running Debian on an SD card has many uses; each user can have their own SD card, specialized systems can be created on their own SD card, SD cards are portable and can be stored in a locked location, and are useful for testing new software. SD card test system backups can be used to quickly produce ready to use test systems.

For systems with an existing OS, the software licenses can be worth more than the hardware. Generally, the Hard drives/SSDs on PCs and Laptops can easily be removed or replaced.

When it comes to multi-OS Systems, running Linux as the primary system and running a secondary OS in a virtual machine can be advantageous. For systems with limited resources, Linux can be run on an SD card indefinitely. Running OSs side by side can result in one OS clobbering the other.

INSTALLING LINUX

This section focuses on safely installing Debian on Intel/ AMD based PCs and Laptops. Download a Debian Live ISO. Create a Debian Live USB stick. Then install Debian.

First, boot the **Debian Live** USB stick. If it fails, stop. Second, install Debian on a removable media such as an SD card, resolve any issues. Third, only if you wish, install Debian on the system's hard drive/SSD.

The **ISO** name comes from the International Organization for Standardization, ISO 9660 standard used for optical disks. The chips use the exact same format.

The methods for creating a Debian Live USB stick from an ISO vary by system. **Balena Etcher** is recommend for Windows. **dd** copy is recommended for Linux and Mac. The **Chromebook Recovery Utility**, is recommended for Chromebooks. The **EtchDroid** app is recommended for Android devices. USB sticks should be 8GB or larger and not SD cards.

The debian.org home page.

The **Debian Live** ISO is not the default **Download** for Debian and has no direct link on the Debian home page. The Debian Live ISO is concealed by a short **ever changing** labyrinth of web pages. Just enough to foster anarchy for writers and new users alike. Before downloading any files, see **Debian Live ISO Install Fails** (Page 6).

Navigating to the Debian Live ISOs

Direct URL to Live ISOs:
cdimage.debian.org/debian-cd/current-live/
amd64/iso-hybrid/

Live CD URL:
debian.org/CD/live/
Under **"stable" release**
   click **Other live ISO**

Navigating from the Home Page:
On the **Debian Home Page**, directly under **Download**
  click **Other downloads**
Under **Try Debian live before installing**.
  click **Other live ISO**
This is subject to change.

From youtube.com/@ruthake:
A direct link to the Debian Live ISOs can be found in the pinned comment for the first video in PC/Laptop playlist.

Current ISO Live Downloads

Scroll down to **debian-live- ... ...-amd64-lxde.iso**.

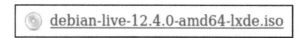

Click the **lxde.iso** link to start the download, version numbers may very.

Debian Live ISO Install Fails

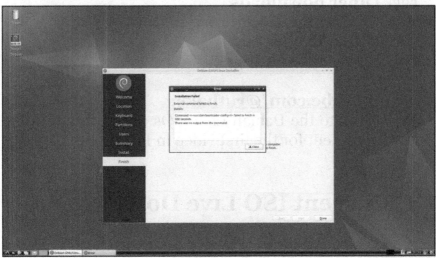

failed to finish in 600 seconds

The **debian-live-12.6.0-amd64-lxde.iso** install failed consistantly at 68% during the filming of the companion videos: Command <i>/usr/sbin/bootloader-config<i> failed to finish in 600 seconds. There was no output from the command.

Same Issue Different Desktop Different Day

Bad ISO Install Workaround

cdimage.debian.org/mirror/cdimage/archive/

Only the Debian/Calamares Team(s) can explain how a defective ISO makes it to publication. Fortunately Debian has a best practice of archiving previous versions.

Navigating the Debian Archive

If the current Live ISO Install fails, a previous ISO can be downloaded from the archive. We have used 12.2.0 without issue: debian-live-12.2.0-amd64-lxde.iso. The Debian archive structure is fairly intuitive:

- cdimage.debian.org/mirror/cdimage/archive/
- 12.2.0-live/
- amd64/
- iso-hybrid/
- debian-live-12.2.0-amd64-lxde.iso

Recommended methods for creating a Debian Live USB stick from an ISO are listed below and vary by system. There are many YouTubes and webpages dedicated to creating ISO image USB sticks.

Windows
1) Balena Etcher
2) UNetbootin

Mac
1) dd copy
2) Balena Etcher
3) UNetbootin

Linux
1) dd copy
2) Balena Etcher
3) UNetbootin

Android
1) EtchDroid

Chromebook
1) Chromebook Recovery Utility

Below **<file>** is the debian-live-12.2.0-amd64-lxde.iso or similarly named file, likely in the **~/Downloads** folder. The USB stick must be unmounted before it can be written to by the **dd** command. The **dd** command shown on two lines below, should be on one line.

Linux dd Copy, from a terminal:

```
df -h
```
df displays mounted partitions. Insert the USB chip. For example, if **sdb1** was mounted, unmount **sdb1**, **sdb** is the device.
```
df -h
umount /dev/sdb1
sudo dd if=~/Downloads/<file>
  of=/dev/sdb bs=4M;sync
```

Mac dd Copy, from a terminal:

```
diskutil list
```
Look for the USB stick.
```
sudo diskutil unmountDisk /dev/disk<#>
sudo dd if=<path/file>
  of=/dev/disk<#> bs=4m,sync
```

Balena Etcher

https://github.com/balena-io/etcher/releases/

Balena manufactures software duplicators for chips. It's multi-platform image software is available from the GitHub site above, etcher.balena.io is it's commercial site.

Balena Etcher

The Balena Etcher software has a very clean streamlined design. The install is also very streamlined. Download the install for your OS. On a Linux system from a terminal:

```
cd ~/Downloads
sudo apt install ./balena-etcher_1.18.11_amd64.deb -y
balena-etcher
```

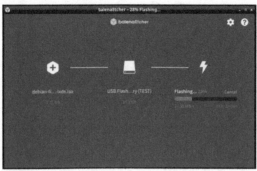

Select the ISO file, select the USB drive, click **Flash**.

Validating after Flashing.

Flash Completed Notification

UNetbootin

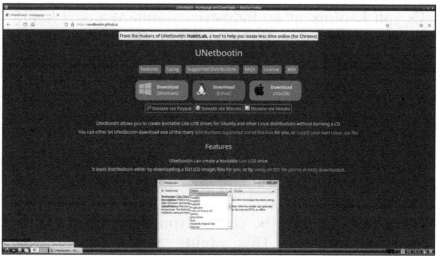

https://unetbootin.github.io

UNetbootin can be downloaded from the GitHub site above, follow the links for your OS.

Select Diskimage, select an ISO, select the USB, click **OK**.

Be patient, this is a slow process. On a Linux system using a FAT32 formatted USB stick, from a terminal:

```
sudo apt install mtools -y
cd ~/Downloads
chmod +x unetbootin-linux-702.bin
sudo ./unetbootin-linux-702.bin
```

Generic Method

PCs and Laptops as an industrial standard have been designed to boot from ISO and FAT32 formatted storage. Debian is distributed using the ISO format. Debian Live ISOs have uses beyond testing and installing Debian, they can be used to create portable systems on a chip as well as full backup systems on a chip, this requires the use of FAT32.

Unfortunately the **Debian Live ISOs** utilize **symlinks** which **FAT32** does not support. **Xarchiver** has historically been able to extract files and translate the full pathways so the files can be copied from an ISO to a FAT32 formatted storage. This ability was removed from Xarchiver with the idea that it would be supported by **ISO Master**. As that failed to happen the ability was restored to Xarchiver in Debian 12. As it turns out **7z** is an excellent **alternative** to **Xarchiver** and **ISO Master**.

A bootable Debian Live USB Stick can be created by using 7z to extract the files from a Debian ISO file and then copying the files to a FAT32 formatted USB stick. As **7z** aka **7-Zip** is multi-platform, this method can by used on virtually any platform. It is important to copy **hidden** files and folder (files an folders starting with a dot) as well (PCManFM Page 45), (Command line: **ls -a** Page 202).

Multi-platform documentation and downloads can be found at 7-zip.org. Wikipedia also has an excellent article on 7-Zip. If **7z** (**p7zip-full**) is not preinstalled with Debian, **p7zip-full** can be installed thru **Synaptic**.

Dash lower case "o" is used to specify the output file path, there is no space between the "o" and the file path. "~" tilde is not recognized by 7z, $HOME is recognized.

Debian Live USB Stick

Creating a **Debian Live USB Stick** using a FAT32 USB stick and 7z:

1. Format a **USB Stick** as **FAT32**.
2. Use **7z** to **extract** the files from the **ISO**.
3. **Copy** the **files** to the **root directory** of the FAT32 USB Stick.
4. **Copy** the **splash images** from the **isolinux** directory to the **boot/grub** directory.

Android & ChromeOS

For Android Devices and ChromeOS based systems running Linux, 7z can be run from the command line:

```
7z x $HOME/Downloads/<debian.iso> -o$HOME/hold
cp ~/hold/isolinux/splash* ~/hold/boot/grub
```

Install: p7zip-full (Should already be installed.)
Documentation: man 7z, 7z --help

If an Android File manager fails with an error while trying to copy all the files at once to a FAT32 formatted USB stick, copy the files one directory at a time and then select the remaining single files and copy them to the FAT32 formatted USB stick. Android devices will create an Android directory structure on the FAT32 USB stick, this wont cause any issues and can be ignored.

Failure to copy the **splash images** will result in a missing image error at boot, press Enter to continue. The GRUB menu will appear in black and white with no background image, this will not affect functionality.

Chromebook Recovery Utility

From the ChromeOS **File** app, right click on the ISO file and select **Zip selection** to create a zipped copy. Using the ChromeOS Chrome browser, install the **Chromebook Recovery Utility** from the Chrome Web Store.

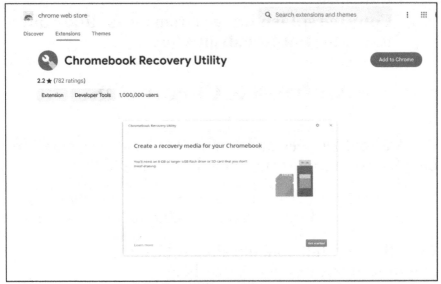

Click **Add to Chrome**

Click **Add extension**

Click the **Extension's** Puzzle Piece icon in the top right and select **Chromebook Recovery Utility**.

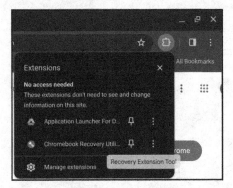

Launch the Chromebook Recovery Utility

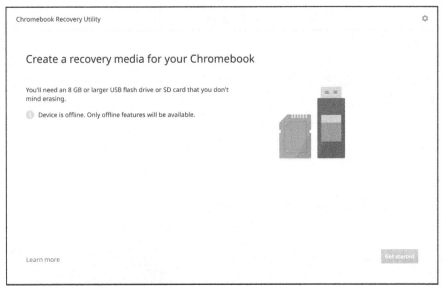

Click the **Gear** icon in the top right corner.

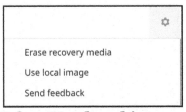

Select **Use local image**.

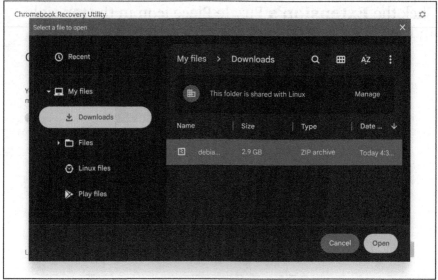

Select the **ZIP**ped file.

Insert the **USB** stick and select it from the pull-down menu then click the **Continue** button.

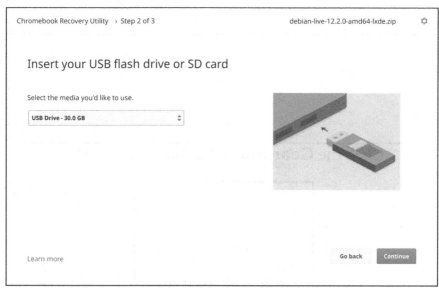

Select the **USB** stick and click **Continue**.

USB stick creation in progress.

The process should complete within a matter of minutes. Click the **Done** button when complete. It is important to **eject** the USB stick from the ChromeOS File app, before removing it.

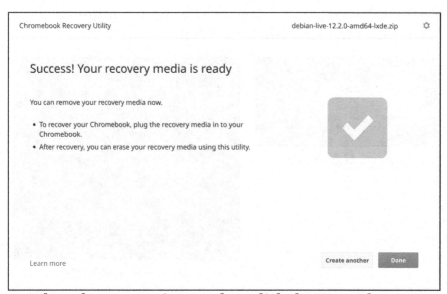

When the process is complete click the **Done** button.

Android EtchDroid

Install EtchDroid from the Google Play Store.

Install **EtchDroid**

Start EtchDroid and select **Write raw image or ISO**. Then select the **ISO file** to be used.

Select **RAW**

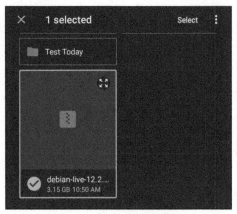

Select the **ISO file**.

Directly under **Select USB drive** click on the **USB stick**. On some Android devices the USB information may be very dark and difficult to read. Regardless, click just under **Select USB drive** to select the **USB drive**.

Select the **USB drive**.

For **Ready to write**, click the **icon** at the bottom right. Then click **OK** to allow access to the USB drive.

For the **Warning**, click **FLASH IMAGE**. Progress can be monitored thru the Notifications.

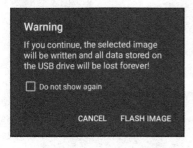

Installing Debian

While booting, most PCs and Laptops will have an option to select a **Boot Menu** which allows the boot device to be selected for the current boot or a **Settings Menu** which allows the boot order to be permanently set. Setting the boot order varies with manufacture and model. Use your cell phone, take a picture before permanently changing the boot order.

Booting Debian Live will not automatically install Debian. Debian can be run as a removable Live version, installed and run on a removable media such as an SD card, or installed directly on the hard drive. As an example Debian will be installed on a Micro SD card connected by a USB to Micro SD card adapter.

Disable Secure Boot, if enabled, when using a Live USB Stick, this process varies with manufacture and model. Insert the Debian Live stick and power on the computer. A menu list will be displayed, press Enter to accept the default selection. Once the Debian desktop is visible, insert the SD card. For any **Removable media is inserted** messages, press the **Cancel** button. Click the **Install Debian** icon, top left.

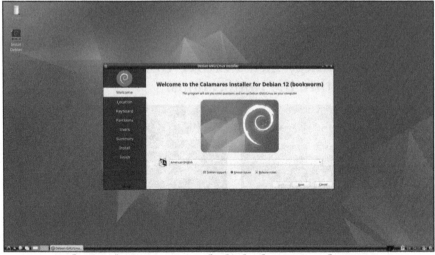

Select a language and click the **Next** button.

Select a Time Zone and click **Next**.

Select a Keyboard and click **Next**.

From the **Select storage device** pull-down select the SD
card, then select **Manual partitioning**. Be careful not to
select the hard drive, unless you mean to.

Select the SD card and click **Next**.

21

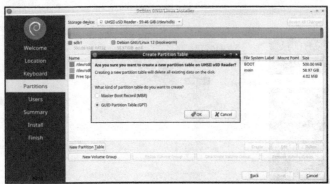

Click the **New Partition Table** button, then click **OK**.

Select the **Free Space** and click the **Create** button.

For Size enter **500**, for File System select **FAT32**, for Mount Point select **/boot/efi**, for FS label enter **boot**, for Flags check **boot**. Click the **OK** button.

For Size use the **default remaining space**, for File System select **ext4**, for Mount Point select /, for FS label enter **main**, do not check any Flags. Click the **OK** button.

Click the **Next** button.

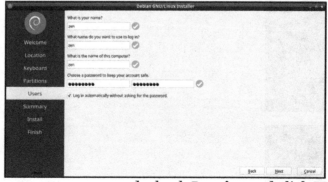

Enter a name, password, check **Log in**, and click **Next**.

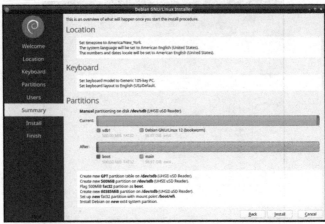

Click **Install** to begin the install

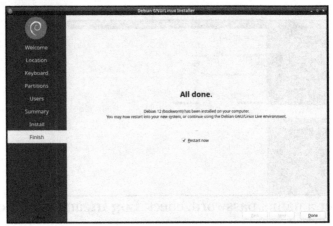

At the **All done** screen, uncheck **Restart now**, and click the **Done** button. Shutdown Debian. Remove the SD card and restart Debian Live. From a terminal:

Menu → System Tools → LXTerminal

```
sudo su
df -h
```

Insert the SD card. For any **Removable media is inserted** messages, press the **OK** button. From the terminal:

```
df -h
```

The difference between the two **df -h** displays is the SD card, this example will use /dev/sdb2. Turn off **ext4 journaling**. From the terminal:

To turn journaling on tune2fs without "^".

```
umount /dev/sdb2
debugfs -R features /dev/sdb2
tune2fs -O ^has_journal /dev/sdb2
debugfs -R features /dev/sdb2
```

Shutdown Debian and remove the Debian Live Stick. Insert the SD card and turn on the computer. There is currently a fixable boot issue, see Page 27. Add three lines to the bottom of **/etc/fstab** From a terminal:

Send tmp and log files to RAM to save read and writes to the SD card.

```
sudo su
cd /etc
cp fstab fstab.bak
nano fstab
  tmpfs /var/log tmpfs defaults,noatime 0 0
  tmpfs /var/tmp tmpfs defaults,noatime 0 0
  tmpfs /tmp     tmpfs defaults,noatime 0 0
```

Ctrl + O, Enter, Ctrl + X

Reboot Debian, the Debian SD card is now ready to use.

Installing Debian on an SD card allows Debian to be tested and any issues resolved before installing it on the computer itself. For newer computers, **Updating the kernel** will generally resolve WiFi, Bluetooth, and screen resolution issues. If the system has internet but is not connecting, see **Network Fix** Page 30. From a terminal:

```
sudo apt update -y
sudo apt dist-upgrade -y
```

Android USB Tethering – can be used to provide internet to a computer. Use a USB cable to connect the phone to the computer. From the Android phone:

Android Settings → Network & internet →
Hotspot & Tethering → **USB tethering**

Updating the kernel – **uname** displays the current kernel version. **apt-cache search** can be used to display kernel options. Look for the latest version. **apt install** can be used to update the kernel, the **image-name** used will have a format similar to the name displayed by the **uname -r** command. From a terminal:

```
uname -r
apt-cache search linux-image | grep "PCs (signed)"
sudo apt install linux-image-<image-name>
```

Shutdown Windows at Boot - While searching for the correct keys to access the boot order of a PC or Laptop with Windows preloaded, Windows may inadvertently be started. To quickly shutdown Windows:

Shift + F10
```
shutdown /s /t 0
```

SD Card Fails to Boot

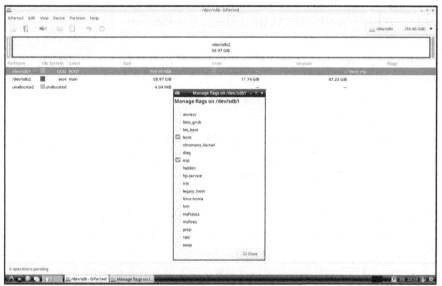

GParted setting partition flags.

Use this procedure if the SD Card fails to boot. With the computer off insert the Debian Live Stick and turn on the computer. Installing GParted will require internet access. Ethernet and USB Tethering (Page 26) tend to work automatically. If WiFi is working, Connman can be used:
Menu → Preferences → Connman Settings

Menu → System Tools → LXTerminal:

```
sudo apt update -y
sudo apt install gparted -y
```

Insert the SD Card and start GParted:
    Menu → System Tools → GParted
From the top right pull-down, select the **SD Card**.
Right click the BOOT partition and select **Manage Flags.**

Click the **boot flag**, the **boot flag** and **esp flag** will be deselected, the **msftdata flag** will be selected. Close GParted and open PCManFM. If any of the SD Card partitions are mounted in PCManFM, eject them. Remove the SD Card for a moment and then reinsert it.

Using PCManFM open the SD Card's **BOOT** partition.
Copy all the files in the **/EFI/Debian** folder
   to the **/EFI/boot** folder.
In the **/EFI/boot** folder
   rename **grubx64.efi** to **BOOTx64.efi**
From the **/EFI/Debian** folder, copy **grubx64.efi**
   to the **/EFI/boot** folder.

Close PCManFM and using GParted, turn the SD Card's BOOT partition **boot flag** back on. This will also turn on the esp flag and turn off the msftdata flag. Close GParted and Shutdown Linux, the Debian Live stick will not retain GParted. The SD Card should now boot without issue.

Forgotten Password Reset

At the **GRUB** menu, press the Cursor Down key then the cursor Up key, to prevent the system from booting.

Press the E key, to edit the startup configuration.
Cursor down to the line that starts with the word **linux**
At the end of the line add **init=/bin/bash**
Press Ctrl + X or F10.
From the terminal:
   Press Enter.
   `mount -o remount,rw /`
   `passwd <user-id>`
   `umount /`
Press Alt + Ctrl + Del.

Three recommendations when running on an SD card:

1) Do not create a Swap Partition.
2) Disable ext4 journaling.
3) Send log and tmp files to RAM.

When the **Erase Disk** option is selected while installing Debian on a hard drive or SSD, a Swap Partition will automatically be configured. This is usually desirable.

Erase Disk auto configuration.

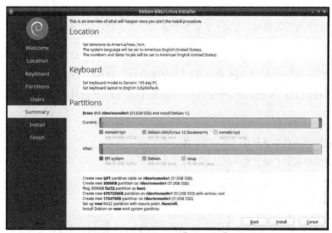

Summary example with SSD .

The LXDE Linux Desktop

Network Fix

If internet has been supplied to the system and yet the system is unable to connect, from a terminal:

```
sudo systemctl restart networking
sudo systemctl restart connman
```

If that fails to work, edit (or create) **/etc/resolv.conf** (resolve without the **e** on the end) file. Below the Google DNS Domain Name Servers are used. From a terminal:

```
sudo nano /etc/resolv.conf
   nameserver 8.8.8.8
   nameserver 8.8.4.4
```
Ctrl + O, Enter, Ctrl + X
Reboot the system.

While deprecated, editing or even deleting resolv.conf and then rebooting appears to resolve some issues.

Customizing the Desktop

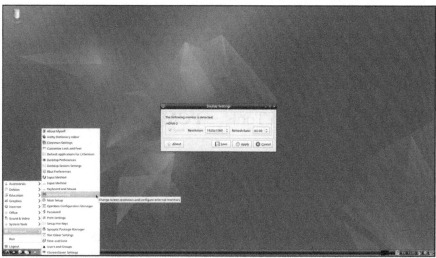

Menu → Preferences → **Monitor Settings**

To set Desktop Preferences: Menu → Preferences or by right clicking on an LXDE component. /usr/share folder contains Wallpapers and Icons. Right click the Desktop:

Desktop Preferences → Appearance tab → **Wallpaper**

Desktop Icons

The Desktop Icon size is set from file manager, PC-ManFM, View → Zoom In/Out. To add an icon to the Desktop, right click the item in the menu and select **Add to desktop**.

Menu → System Tools → **PCManFM**

LXDE Font Settings

LXDE font settings can be found in a few spots:

Menu → Preferences → Customize Look and Feel
    Widget tab: Default font
    Window Border tab:
     Title Bar sub tab:
       Font for active window title
       Font for inactive window title
     Misc. sub tab:
       Font for menu header
       Font for menu Item
       Font for on-screen display
       Font for inactive on-screen display

Right click on the Taskbar → Panel Settings
    Appearance tab:
     Font

Right click on the Desktop → Desktop Preferences
    Appearance tab:
     Text

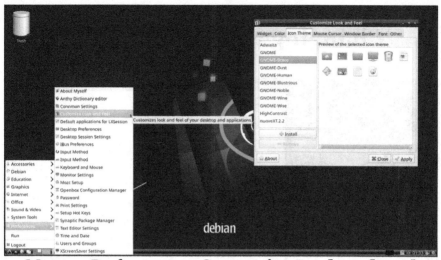

Menu → Preferences → **Customize Look and Feel**

The system's icon style can be selected from the Customize Look and Feel **Icon Theme** tab. The practice of decorating and customizing a Desktop is often referred to as "Ricing". There are many YouTubes and webpages dedicated to the fine art of Ricing. The menu icon itself can also be changed. Icons can be edited and additional icons and themes can be added.

Right click the Menu Icon, select **"Menu" Settings**.

Changing a Program's Icon

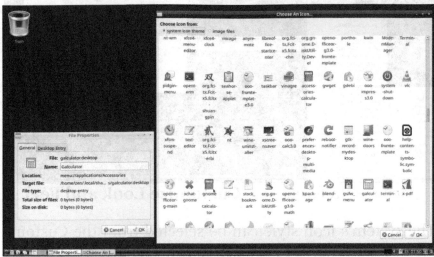

Selecting a new icon.

To change a program's icon, right click the menu item and select **Properties**. In the **File Properties** window click the program's icon, the **Choose An Icon** window opens. Select an icon and click the Ok button.

Screensaver

To turn off the LXDE Screensaver:
    LXDE Menu → Preferences → XScreenSaver Settings
    For **Mode** select **Disable Screen Saver.**

Screenshots

Screenshots by default are saved in the Pictures folder in the users home folder, ~/Pictures. Press **Print Screen** to take a screenshot or: Menu → Accessories → **Screenshot**

LXDE TASKBAR

The LXDE Taskbar can be can be colored, styled, and repositioned. There can be more than one panel and applets can be added and removed from the Taskbar.

LXDE Taskbar Defaults

The LXDE Taskbar can easily be reset to it's default settings by deleting the lxpanel directory and then rebooting Linux. This is also useful if the Taskbar is accidentally deleted. To reset the LXDE Taskbar to it's default values, from Terminal:

```
cd ~/.config
rm -r lxpanel
```

Shutdown and restart Linux.

Panel Preferences

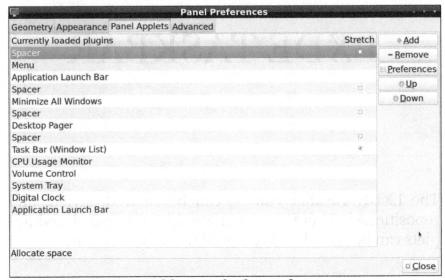

Taskbar Default Applets

The LXDE Taskbar is feature rich and easy to configure. Right click on the **Taskbar** and select **Add / Remove Panel Items**. The **Panel Preferences** panel opens with the **Panel Applets** tab selected. All the panel settings can be set from here. To change an applets settings, select it and click the **Preferences** button. Applets can be moved left and right along the Taskbar using the **Up** and **Down** buttons. Select an applet and click the **Remove** button to delete it.

The **Resource monitors** plugin is a nice replacement for **CPU Usage Monitor**, and allows color settings.

Add Plugin to Panel

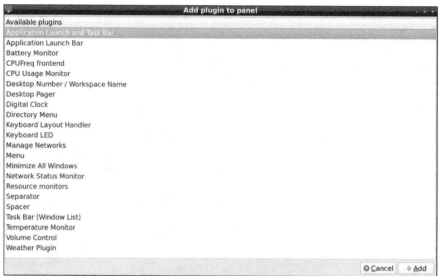

Available Panel Plugins

Clicking the **Add** button opens the **Add plugin to panel** panel, which shows a full list of Taskbar applet plugins. Select an applet and click the **Add** button to add it to the Taskbar.

Application Launch Bar

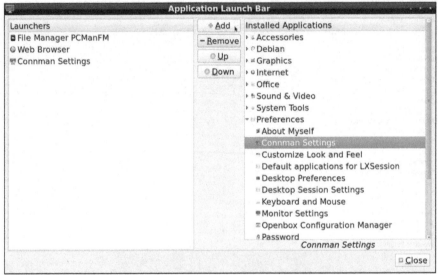

Application Launch Bar Editor

Programs can be added/pinned or removed/unpinned from an **Application Launch Bar**. From the **Panel Preferences**, **Panel Applets tab**, select the **Application Launch Bar** on the left and click the **Preferences** button. The **Application Launch Bar** panel opens. To pin, select an application from the right side then press the **Add** button. To unpin, select an application from the left side then press the **Remove** button.

Preferences button

Task Bar (Window List) Preferences

The taskbar's appearance can be set from the Panel Preferences **Appearance** tab. Setting the font color will for example change the clock font color. To include the open **Window List,** from **Panel Applets** tab, select **Task Bar (Window List)**, click the **Preferences** button, and check the **Flat buttons** option.

The Digital Clock can be changed from a 24 hour display to a 12 hour display. From the **Panel Applets** tab, select the **Digital Clock** and click the **Preferences** button. Change **Clock Format** from %R to %I:%M %p. For more clock format options, from a terminal: date --help.

Advanced Settings

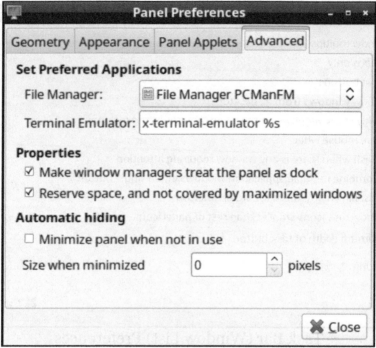

Advanced tab

The **Panel Preferences**, **Advanced tab** allows the default **file manager** and **terminal** to be selected. A reboot is required for changes to take affect. Menu items that launch from a terminal will use the selected terminal. Taskbar **Automatic hiding** can be fine tuned and enabled here.

Add Connman to the Taskbar

Edit the **Connman launch command**.

Menu → Preferences → Right click **Connman Settings**
Select **Properties**
Select the **Desktop Entry** tab.
Change the **Command:**
   From: connman-gtk
   To: connman-gtk --no-icon
Click the **OK** button.

Pin the **Connman Settings** program to the Application Launch Bar, see Page 38.

From the **Application Launch Bar** panel:
Expand **Preferences** on the right side.
Select **Connman Settings**.
Click the **Add** button.
Click the **Close** button.

Add the **Network Status Monitor** plugin to the Taskbar, see Page 37.

From the **Add plugin to panel** panel:
Select the **Network Status Monitor**.
Click the **Add** button.
Click the **Close** button.

Note: Connman connection profiles are located:
   /var/lib/connman/**<profile-folder>**

Connman

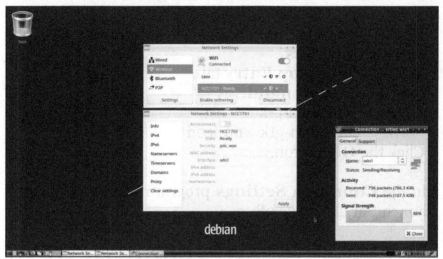

Connman and Network Status Monitor Settings

Clicking **Connman** in the **Application Launch Bar** opens the Connman **Network Settings**. The type of network can be selected on the left. The specific network can be selected on the right. Clicking the gear to the right of the network name allows specific settings for that network to be set. Clicking on the **Network Status Monitor** opens the opens the **Connection Properties** window. The Network Status Monitor **name** must be set to the same name as the Connman Network Settings **Interface** (name) in order for it to work (**wlo1** above).

BASIC SETUP

Linux is unique in that every part of it is accessible to the user. With understanding, access is control. With that control the system can be molded to the vision of the user.

The terminal is the CLI, Command-Line Interface to the operating system. It is the most important access point of the system. The command-line is not something to be feared, it's not that easy to enter a wrong command that will do damage.

Knowledge is power and Linux is loaded with documentation. Debian, doubly so, empowering it's users with the the documentation details they need.

Access that goes all the way down to the source code of the programs that make up a distro. Allowing programs to be studied and modified without limit, full control.

Whether it's distros, desktops, or applications, Linux is all about choice. The freedom of choice, freedom from forced updates, freedom to explore, and free as in free from fees.

LXTerminal

Terminals are the Command Line Interface, CLI, to the operating system. Most Linux terminals will speak BASH short for Bourne Again SHell, also referred to as a BASH terminal. **echo $0** (zero) and **ps** can be used to displays the terminal's language.

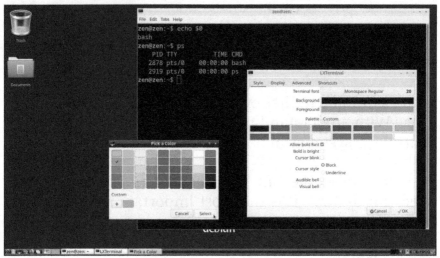

Edit → Preferences

To customize LXTerminal, select **Preferences** from the **Edit** menu. Click the color block to the right of **Background** and **Foreground** to change their color. Click the block to the right of **Terminal font**, select a font and font size, then click the **Select** button. When done click the **OK** button.

Ctrl + Shift + +   Temporarily increase font size.
Ctrl + Shift + −   Temporarily decrease font size.
Ctrl + L   Clear the screen.

PCManFM

Menu → System Tools → File Manager PCManFM

F11 is the full screen toggle. Ctrl + H is the hidden file toggle, files that start with a dot. Ctrl + D bookmarks the location. F3 for Dual Panel Mode. Pressing Delete while a file or folder is selected sends it to the **Trash Can,** Shift + Delete deletes the file or folder. Ctrl + Q to Quit.

Changing the icon size, View → **Zoom In / Zoom Out**, also changes the Desktop icon size. PCManFM can also launch programs, Go → Applications.

To display all image previews regardless of size, Edit → Preferences → **Display** tab, **Do not generate thumbnails for files exceeding this size:** set to 0 (Zero).

To set the default application for a file, right click the file and select **Open With...** select the application or enter a custom command, check the **Set selected application as default action for this file type** checkbox. Click the **OK** button.

When running a Root File Manger, it's a good practice to change the icon theme (GNOME-Wine). From a terminal:
```
sudo pcmanfm
```

Mousepad

Mousepad can be very plain.

Menu → Accessories → Mousepad
Edit → **Preferences**

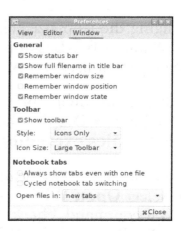

F11 is the full screen toggle. **Ctrl** + **Q** to quit. **Ctrl** + **F** to find. **Ctrl** + **R** to find and replace. Document → Filetype can be used to manually select the type of syntax highlighting, **Plain Text** for no highlighting. **Ctrl** + **P** to print. Selected **Print to File** to print to PDF.

Mousepad Configured

```
File Edit Search View Document Help

54     else
55         color_prompt=
56     fi
57 fi
58
59 if [ "$color_prompt" = yes ]; then
60     PS1='${debian_chroot:+($debian_chroot)}\[\033[01;32m\]\u@\h\[\033[00m\]:\[\033[01;34m\]\w\[\033[00m\]\
61 else
62     PS1='${debian_chroot:+($debian_chroot)}\u@\h:\w\$ '
63 fi
64 unset color_prompt force_color_prompt
65
66 # If this is an xterm set the title to user@host:dir
67 case "$TERM" in
68 xterm*|rxvt*)
69     PS1="\[\e]0;${debian_chroot:+($debian_chroot)}\u@\h: \w\a\]$PS1"
70     ;;
71 *)
72     ;;
73 esac
74

                                    Filetype: sh  UTF-8  Line: 67 Column: 15  OVR
```

Mousepad Configured

paperconf will display the current system default paper size. **paperconf -a** will display all available paper sizes. **paperconfig -p** sets the default paper size, from a terminal:

```
sudo su
cat /etc/papersize
paperconf
paperconf -a
paperconfig -p letter
paperconf
man paperconf          Cursor Up / Down.
man paperconfig        Q to quit man.
exit
```

To open a text file in Mousepad while using PCManFM, right click the file and select Mousepad. It is a good practice to use a different **Color scheme** for the **Root** user, as a reminder to self the Root id is being used.

APT – Software

Description: APT - Advanced Packaging Tool. Attempting to **install** an already installed package will have no affect. In addition to being able to search and download from the Debian repositories, APT can directly install dot deb software package files offered by some websites:

```
sudo apt install ./<file-name>.deb
```

Most used, prefix with sudo:

apt update	update package list
apt dist-upgrade	upgrade the OS
apt upgrade	upgrade everything
apt full-upgrade	upgrade with delete
apt list <name>	search by name
apt search <desc>	search descriptions
apt search ^<desc>$	exact match
apt show <name>	show package details
apt install <name>	install package
apt remove <name>	remove package
apt satisfy <name>	satisfy dependencies

Documentation: man apt, apt --help

CLI: apt --help

Command-Line Help

Terminals generally use the cursor Up / Down keys to roll thru previous commands, which can then be edited. **man**, **info** and **less** also use the cursor Up / Down keys, Q to quit. **history** provides a list of previously entered commands. ~ (tilde, just under the Esc key) is short for **$HOME**, the users home directory. If a program is already installed, doing anther **apt install** will not do anything or cause any harm. Programs may not have a man, info, or --help option (generally a quick reference). Programs may have their own built-in help. From a terminal:

```
sudo apt install less -y
sudo apt install info -y
sudo apt install htop -y
sudo apt install neofetch -y
sudo apt install screenfetch -y
sudo apt install gpick -y
sudo apt install wm-icons -y
sudo apt install x11-xserver-utils -y
sudo apt install xterm -y
history
help                    Help for built-in commands.
man history             Cursor Up / Down, Q to quit.
man man
man --help
man info
info man
info
echo $HOME
echo ~                  Same as:  echo $HOME
env                     List environmental variables.
env --help
man env
```

XTerm

XTerm is configured by creating a (dot) .Xresoureces file in the home directory. **x11-xserver-utils** is required to make this work. **faceSize** sets the font size. For XTerm settings to take effect the **xrdb -merge** command must be run and if XTerm is already running, it must be restarted. To copy text: Hold down the left mouse button down while dragging the mouse over the text to be copied. Release the left mouse button, then press both mouse buttons at the same time and then release them. To paste, press Shift + Insert From a terminal:

```
nano ~/.Xresources
  xterm*saveLines: 2000
  xterm*loginShell: true
  xterm*selectToClipboard: true
  xterm*faceName: Monospace
  xterm*faceSize: 12
  xterm*Foreground: SlateBlue1
  xterm*Background: black
  xterm*pointerColor: red3
  xterm*cursorColor: red3
Ctrl + O, Enter, Ctrl + X
  xrdb -merge ~/.Xresources
  xterm --help
  man xterm
```

Ctrl + L	Clear the screen.
ALT + Enter	Fullscreen Toggle
Shift + PageUp	Roll up screen.
Shift + PageDown	Roll down screen.

Menu → System Tools → XTerm

htop is a system monitor. **screenfetch** and **neofetch** display information about the system. The pipe "|", pipes the output of one command into the next command. **grep** searches for key words, use quotes when spaces are used. **clear**, clears the display. From XTerm:

```
man htop
Q
htop --help
htop
Q
history | less
Q
history | grep htop
clear
screenfetch
Ctrl + L
Alt + Enter
neofetch
Alt + Enter
exit
```

Colors

Two common ways to express color in Linux are to use a color name or a six digit hex red, green, blue, coding scheme. 000000 is black, FFFFFF is white, FF0000 is red, 00FF00 is green, FF00FF is purple. Hex uses 0 thru 9 plus A, B, C, D, E, and F. 2A hex = 2x16 + 10 = 42. FF = 255, so there are 255 to the third power possible colors, over 16 million colors..

Gpick is one of many color selection tools available thru Linux. It can provide identity values for sampled and manually selected colors. Even generate color wheel complementary, analogous, triadic, split-complementary, rectangle, square, neutral, clash, and five and six tone schemes.

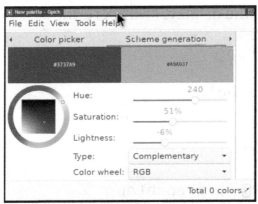

Menu → Graphics → Gpick

showrgb is a CLI tool that lists colors by name and shows decimal rgb values. From a terminal:

```
showrgb | less
showrgb | grep red
```

Galculator and Xcalc can be used to convert decimal to hexidecimal.

Audio

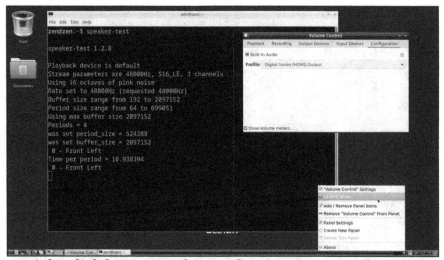

Right click bottom right speaker icon → Launch Mixer

It's not uncommon to have to select the audio profile to enable audio. **speaker-test** provides pink noise which can be used for troubleshooting audio issues. The pink noise sounds like static when switching between radio stations. If the TV/Monitor and Linux volumes are at moderate levels and there is no sound, it will likely be necessary to select an Audio **Profile** from the **Mixer**. To start a speaker test, from a terminal:

```
sudo apt install alsa-utils -y
speaker-test    Closing the terminal ends the test.
```

To launch the **Mixer**, right click the Taskbar **Speaker** icon in the lower right of the screen. Select **Launch Mixer**. Enlarge the screen or scroll to the right until the **Configuration** tab is visible. From the pull down select the profile for your system. Trying profiles will not cause any harm. If the speaker-test times out, restart it.

Xrandr

```
zen@zen:~$ xrandr
Screen 0: minimum 320 x 200, current 1920 x 1080, maximum 16384 x 16384
HDMI-1 disconnected primary (normal left inverted right x axis y axis)
HDMI-2 connected 1920x1080+0+0 (normal left inverted right x axis y axis) 880mm x 490mm
   1920x1080     60.00*+  50.00    59.94    24.00    23.98
   1680x1050     59.88
   1600x900      60.00
   1280x1024     75.02
   1440x900      59.90
   1360x768      60.02
   1152x864      75.00
   1280x720      60.00    50.00    59.94
   1024x768      75.03    70.07    60.00
   800x600       72.19    75.00    60.32    56.25
   720x576       50.00
   720x480       60.00    59.94    59.94
   640x480       75.00    72.81    60.00    59.94
   720x400       70.08
zen@zen:~$ xrandr --output HDMI-2 --rotate normal
zen@zen:~$ xrandr --output HDMI-2 --rotate left
zen@zen:~$ xrandr --output HDMI-2 --rotate normal
zen@zen:~$
```

Xrandr showing HDMI-2

Menu → Preferences → **Monitor Settings**, provides basic configuration for monitors. Xrandr is used for more complex monitor configures, multi-monitors, orientation, and arrangement. The Xrander configuration will be lost when the system is rebooted. BASH scripts are a convenient way to save and run Xrander commands.

From a terminal, replace HDMI-2 with your monitor:

```
man xrandr
Q
xrandr -help
xrandr
xrandr --output HDMI-2 --rotate normal
xrandr --output HDMI-2 --rotate left
xrandr --output HDMI-2 --rotate normal
```

After **rotate left** tap the Cursor Up key twice to recall **rotate normal**.

ARandR

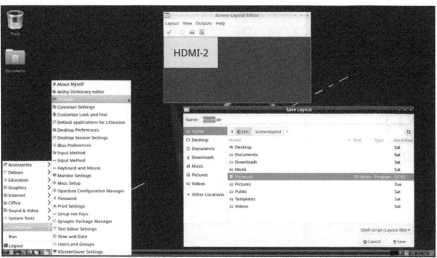

Menu → Preferences → ARandR

From a terminal:

```
sudo apt install arandr -y
```

ARandR is a GUI frontend for Xrandr. ARandR will not directly make any changes. ARandR generates a BASH script (.sh file) with the Xrandr commands in it. Running the script executes the Xrandr commands. Left click and hold on a monitor while dragging to reposition it. Right click on a monitor to change the orientation or resolution. To name and save the configuration:

Layout → Save As → myres.sh

Before setting up the ARandR script to run at startup, it's a good practice to test the script by running it. As an example to run myres.sh, from a terminal:

```
./myres.sh
sudo reboot
```
./ means this directory
If there are issues reboot.

55

Autostart

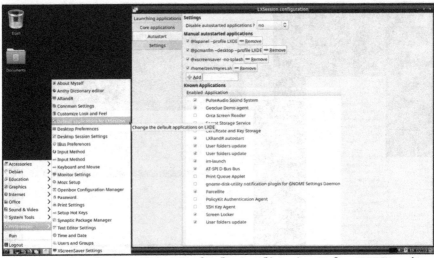

Menu → Preferences → Default applications for LXSession

It's convenient to run the BASH script created by ARandR automatically when the system is started. The **Default applications for LXSession** eases this process. Select the **Autostart** tab, enter the full path to the script and click the **Add** button. The "~" tilde character can not be used in the path. To remove the BASH script from **Autostart**, click the **Remove** button. It's a good practice to take a screenshot of the **Autostart** tab before making any changes. The ARandR BASH script is a plain text file and can be viewed and edited like any other text file.

From a terminal:
   `cat myres.sh`   View the ARandR script with cat.

/usr/share/applications and ~/.local/share/applications <name>.desktop files copied to ~/.config/autostart will start with the Desktop.

Menu Launch Commands

When a program's **launch command** is edited in the **menu** it is copied before it is modified. It's copied:

From:
   /usr/share/applications   Never edit these.
To:
   ~/.local/share/applications/   Ok to edit or delete.

{dot}.desktop files in the ~/.local/share/applications/ directory can be edited or deleted without causing any harm, they are override files. If they are deleted, the menu lists will return to what they were before the file was created.

Adding a Menu Entry

The move command, **mv,** can be used to rename files in ~/.local/share/applications. This causes the /usr/share/applicatons entry to reappear in the menu.
Right click Firefox, Menu → Internet → **Firefox ESR**
Select **Properties**
   On the **General** tab:
      Click the **icon** and select a new one.
      Change the **Name:** to **Terminal**
   On the **Desktop Entry** tab:
      Change the **Command:** to **lxterminal**
   Click the **OK** button.
Menu → Internet → **Terminal**   Firefox is gone.
```
cd ~/.local/share/applications
mv firefox-esr.desktop test.desktop
```
Menu → Internet → Firefox   Firefox is back.

Bluetooth

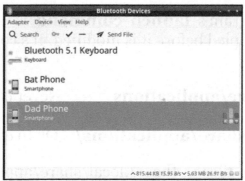

Menu → Preferences → Bluetooth Manager

From a terminal:

```
sudo apt install blueman -y
```

Reboot after installing Blueman. Bluetooth can be started from the menu or by right clicking on the Bluetooth icon in the System Tray. As connecting Bluetooth devices grants access to your system, there will be questions asking to accept, enable or confirm.

The **Bluetooth Devices** menu is the primary menu, where devices can be paired and then connected. When pairing a new device, it may be helpful to temporarily set the system to **Always visible** in the **Bluetooth Adapters** menu.

To turn off autostart; right click the **Bluetooth tray icon**, select the **Plugins** menu, on the left side scroll down to and select **PowerManager**, click the **Configuration** button on the right side, and uncheck **Auto power-on**. Bluetooth must also be turned off in **Connman**.

Bluetoothctl

Bluetoothctl is a command-line option for working with Bluetooth devices. It's **default-agent** is useful for sending a **pin** when working with problematic devices like Logitech Bluteoooth keyboards. From a terminal:

```
bluetoothctl --help
bluetoothctl
help
discoverable on
pairable on
scan on
pair <dev>
connect <dev>
exit
```

Bluetooth Issues

Missing new equipment device drivers are the most common Bluetooth issue. **dmesg** may provide helpful hints. Do **NOT** install drives from unknown sources. An internet search on the **model**, **manufacture**, and **bluetooth** is often helpful. Below, **dmesg** shows a missing 0040-1050 driver. **ln -s** creates a symbolic link routing requests for the 0040-1050 driver to 1040-4150.

Beelink s12 Pro / Intel N100, solution:

```
sudo su
 dmesg | grep bluetooth
 cd /usr/lib/firmware/intel
 ln -s ibt-1040-4150.ddc ibt-0040-1050.ddc
 ln -s ibt-1040-4150.sfi ibt-0040-1050.sfi
```

Desktop Shortcut

Creating a Downloads folder Desktop Link

Links to documents, files and folders can be added to the desktop for quick access. This allows a document to remain where it is while providing Desktop access with a double click. The default application should be set for a file type (Page 45). Desktop links can be deleted without affecting the actual document.

Create a Downloads folder Desktop link:

> Menu → System Tools → **PCManFM**
> Select **Home Folder** on the left.
> Click the **Downloads** folder on the right.
> Edit → **Create Link...**
> From the **Select Folder** window:
>   Select **Desktop** on the left.
> Click the **OK** button.

LXDE Keyboard Shortcuts

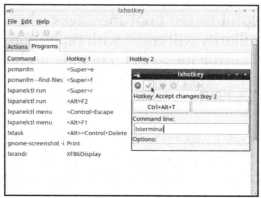

Menu → Preferences → Setup Hot Keys

LXDE keyboard shortcuts can be viewed or edited from **Setup Hot Keys**. Create a shortcut to start LXTerminal:

Menu → Preferences → **Setup Hot Keys**
   Select the **Programs** tab
   Edit → **New**
   Click inside the **Hotkey 1** box
   Alt + **Ctrl** + **T**
   Command line: **lxterminal**
   Click the **Checkmark** to accept the change.
   File → **Save**

To Remove a program shortcut:
   From the **Programs** tab
   Click on the shortcut to highlight it.
   Edit → **Delete**
   File → **Save**

Startup Messages

It can be helpful to see boot messages when a system is starting. Familiarity will come with repetition. It's normal to see various error messages. Looking up boot messages is good learning experience. If the system displays an error message and fails to boot, the error is likely the cause.

To see the boot messages, edit the GRUB file and comment out the "**quiet splash**" line by placing a # at start of the line. Reboot for the change to take affect.

From a terminal:

```
sudo su
cd /etc/default
cp grub grub.bak
nano grub
   # GRUB_CMDLINE_LINUX_DEFAULT="quiet splash"
Ctrl + O, Enter, Ctrl + X
update-grub
```

Debian Handbook

Download the **Debian Handbook** from a terminal:

```
sudo apt install debian-handbook -y
```

From Firefox, enter the url **file:///** and navigate to:

/usr/share/doc/debian-handbook/html/en-US/index.html

SYNAPTIC

The Synaptic Package Manager installs with the LXDE Desktop and is not bias toward any particular desktop making it a good fit for LXDE. Synaptic provides a GUI frontend to the APT package management system, providing easy access to thousands of programs.

When the Debian repositories are updated, it may be necessary to do an **update** and **dist-upgrade** from the command line:

```
sudo apt update -y
sudo apt dist-upgrade -y
```

Sandbox message can safely be ignored. For actual errors, Synaptic will usually provide the command necessary to resolve the issue.

Synaptic is a GUI front-end for APT. For an example APT sources.list file see Page 66.

Synaptic Package Manager

Start Synaptic:
LXDE Menu → Preferences → Synaptic Package Manager

Synaptic has six sections, a menu and toolbar at the top, a status bar at the bottom, search groups on the left, a software package list on the right and below that the software package description. The center sections can be resized. It is important from time to time to update the package information by pressing **Reload** (toolbar top left). **Search** (toolbar top right) searches the entire software package list by keyword. The software package list can be scrolled, paged, or will jump to a software package as you type out it's name. Clicking on a packing will highlight it, double clicking will offer to mark it for install. Highlighted software packages can be marked for install by pressing the Spacebar or Enter key. Pressing **Apply** (toolbar) will install the software package. Synaptic warnings can safely be ignored, they are informational. An actual error message will usually provide a solution.

Install cmatrix with Synaptic

Click **Search** in the toolbar, top right.
In the search box enter: **cmatrix**
Press the **Search** button.
Double click on **cmatrix** in the package list.
In the "Mark additional required changes" pop up:
Click the **Mark** button.
Click **Apply** in the toolbar.
In the "Apply the following changes?" pop up:
Click the **Apply** button.
In the "Changes applied" pop up:
Click the **Close** button.
Synaptic will update.
Click **Properties** in the toolbar.
Maximize the **cmatrix Properties** pop up window.
Click the "**Installed Files**" tab.
Useful for finding program names and file locations.
   /usr/bin/cmatrix
Close Synaptic.

Explore the cmatrix program loaded from Synaptic.
which shows a program's location. Q to quit cmatrix.
From Terminal:

```
which cmatrix
man cmatrix
```

```
cmatrix
```

For the purposes of this book, when using **Search** (toolbar top right) from the **Look in** pull-down select **Name**.

Finding Installed Files

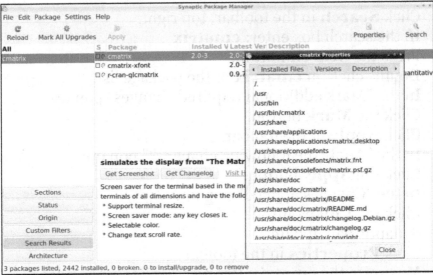

cmatrix File Locations

If there is an issues locating installed files, Synaptic can help. From **Synaptic**, select the package, click on **Properties** in the toolbar, top right. Roll left and right to find the **Installed Files** tab, click on the **Installed Files** tab to see where files may be stored.

Example: /etc/apt/sources.list file:

See https://wiki.debian.org/SourcesList for more information.
deb http://deb.debian.org/debian bookworm main non-free-firmware
deb-src http://deb.debian.org/debian bookworm main non-free-firmware

deb http://deb.debian.org/debian bookworm-updates main non-free-firmware
deb-src http://deb.debian.org/debian bookworm-updates main non-free-firmware

deb http://security.debian.org/debian-security/ bookworm-security main non-free-firmware
deb-src http://security.debian.org/debian-security/ bookworm-security main non-free-firmware

Backports allow you to install newer versions of software made available for this release
deb http://deb.debian.org/debian bookworm-backports main non-free-firmware
deb-src http://deb.debian.org/debian bookworm-backports main non-free-firmware

SOFTWARE

"If you don't like it, fork it.", is a cornerstone of Linux. Linux, often called GNU Linux, is packaged, distributed, as a Distro, a Linux Distribution, a Collection of Linux Software. A visit to the distrowatch.com website can provide an idea of how many Distros exist. This chapter provides a taste of what Linux has to offer. It is important to note, not every app will work on every computer.

Debian provides convenient access to source code. This is an opportunity to learn from existing programs or modify them to meet specific needs (Page 156).

The Linux From Scratch, LFS Project provides step-by-step instructions for building a Linux system. Learn how Linux works by building a Linux system. Learn more at: linuxfromscratch.org

It's a good practice to test new software on a test chip before installing on a primary storage system. This can also help to determine if there is a software conflict. Always backup a system before installing new software, Page 241.

Firefox – Web Browser

Firefox

Install: Installs with LXDE.

Description: Web Browser. To set as default: Firefox Settings → General → Startup, click the **Make default** button. (See also Pages 179 - 181)

F11 - Full Screen toggle   Ctrl + P - Print
Ctrl + D - Bookmark   Ctrl + S - Save Page
                                             F12 - Developer Tools

Special URL's:
         about:about   - List of Special URL's
         about:config   - Browser Flags
         file:///   - File System Browser

Documentation: man firefox-esr, firefox --help
                            Built-in Help, Websites, YouTubes

LXDE: Menu → Internet → Firefox ESR
i3wm: fir – Firefox ESR

Chromium – Web Browser

Chromium

Install: chromium

Description: Web Browser. To set as default: Settings →
Default browser → click the **Make default** button.

F11 - Full Screen toggle   Ctrl + P - Print
Ctrl + D - Bookmark   Ctrl + S - Save Page
                                      F12 - Developer Tools

Special URL's:
         chrome://about   - List of Special URL's
         chrome://flags   - Browser Flags
         file:///   - File System Browser

Documentation: man chromium, chromium --help
                        Built-in Help, Websites, YouTubes

LXDE: Menu → Internet → Chromium Web Browser
i3wm: chr – Chromium Web Browser

Surf – Web Browser

Surf

Install: surf, apparmor-utils

Description: Apparmor must be set to **complain** in order to use the Surf web browser. See Apparmor Page 240. See Adding a Menu Entry Page 57.

Before using Surf, from a terminal:
```
sudo aa-complain /usr/bin/surf
```

Ctrl + H - Back History
Ctrl + L - Forward History
F11 - Full Screen Toggle.

Documentation: man surf, surf --help, YouTubes

CLI: surf start.duckduckgo.com   or any webpage
      surf file:///   or any html document

Text Based Browsers

Install: lynx, w3m (Optional: w3m-img)

Description: Fast, efficient, low bandwidth, can filter ads, and can be used to automate tasks. Text browsers are geared toward technical users. It is not uncommon to set the user agent.

Documentation: man lynx, lynx --help, man w3m, w3m --help. lynx and w3m YouTubes.

CLI: lynx, w3m

Know Your Website

Use **dig** and **whois** to find out more about a website. **traceroute** shows how many hops and how long it takes to reach a site. "Whatweb" can provide detailed technical information on a website and has over 900 plugins. "Netcat" is multi-tool, with many YouTubes dedicated to it.

Install: bind9-dnsutils, whois, traceroute

From LXTerminal:

```
dig google.com
whois google.com
traceroute google.com
Ctrl + C                        If needed.
```

Networks

Modern networks assign an address to a device much like an apartment building address. Device port numbers are like apartment numbers. For an address like https:// 127.0.0.1:631 an IPv4 formatted address, https is the scheme (purpose), :631 is the port, 127.0.0.1 is the web address. To see how you appear to the internet, visit google.com or start.duckduckgo.com and search on "**my ip**" and "**my user agent**". IPV6 is the new standard. The user agent is your browser and OS information.

Firefox allows a User Agent to be set manually, it is preferable not to change this. Display the User Agent from Firefox: Firefox Menu → More Tools → Web Developer Tools Select the Console tab Enter:

```
navigator.userAgent
```

hostname -I shows the network addresses of the host. **ip add show** will show all network addresses. **lsof** can be used to show all open ports. **grep** is used to **filter** the output.

From LXTerminal:

```
hostname -I
ip add show
sudo lsof -i -P -n | grep LISTEN
```

Pidgin – IM Chat

Pidgin

Install: pidgin

Example using Bonjour protocol:

Bonjour chat sessions are serverless, but must be on the same network.

From the Pidgin Accounts window (Ctrl + A):
    Click the **Add** button.
    From the Protocol pull down select **Bonjour**.
    Enter a Username.
    Click the **Add** button.

LXDE: Menu → Internet → Pidgin Internet Messenger
i3wm: pi - Pidgin Internet Messenger

LibreOffice – Office Suite

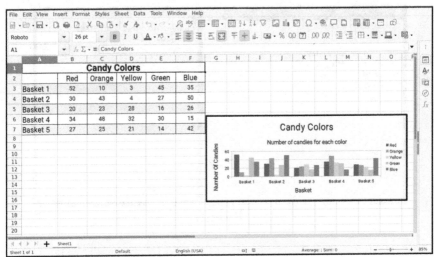

LibreOffice - Calc

Install: LibreOffice installs with LXDE.

Description: Word Processing, Spreadsheet,
Desktop Publishing

Documentation: Built-in Help, libreoffice.org, YouTubes

LXDE: Menu → Office → LibreOffice
i3wm: li - LibreOffice

Set LibreOffice Language:
From **Synaptic** search by **Name** for **libreoffice-help**
and **libreoffice-l10n** (lower case l as in Libre, number
10) install both files for the desired languages.
Menu → Office → **LibreOffice**
Tools → **Options**
Language Settings → Languages
Language of User Interface → select language

Clipart – LibreOffice

LibreOffice Draw with Gallery Open

Install: openclipart-libreoffice

Description: LibreOffice installs with LXDE. Clip art can be added from the View or Insert menu:
    View → Gallery
    Insert → Image...

File Location: /usr/share/openclipart/png/
                     /usr/share/openclipart/svg/

To add MS Core fonts see Page 272.

Math – LibreOffice

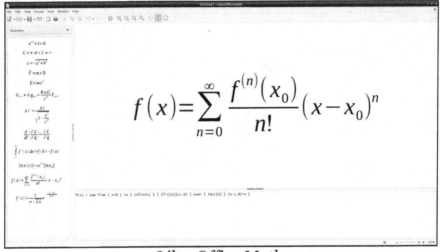

LibreOffice Math

Install: LibreOffice installs with LXDE.

Description: LibreOffice Math is used to create complex mathematical documentation.

Documentation: Built-in Help, libreoffice.org, YouTubes

LXDE: Menu → Office → LibreOffice - Math
i3wm: mat – LibreOffice Math

MuseScore – Music Composition

MuseScore – Composition and Notation

Install: musescore

Description: Music composition and notation
program.

Documentation: Built-in Help, YouTubes,
musescore.org

LXDE: Menu → Sound & Video → MuseScore 2
i3wm: mus – musescore

GIMP – Bitmap Graphics

GIMP

Install: gimp, gimp-data-extras, gimp-help-en, gimp-lensfun, gimp-plugin-registry, gimp-texturize

Description: Edit photos and other bitmap graphics.

Documentation: Built-In Help, Websites, gimp.org, YouTubes, Books

LXDE: Menu → Graphics → GNU Image Manipulation Program

i3wm: gn - GNU Image Manipulation Program

Inkscape – Vector Graphics

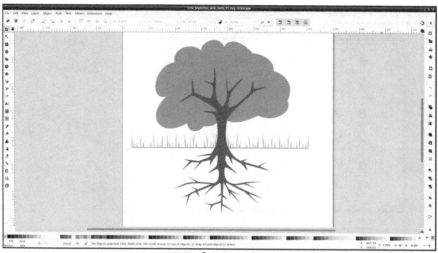

Inkscape

Install: inkscape, inkscape-tutorials

Description: Create and edit vector graphics.

Documentation: Built-in Help, Help → Tutorials, Books
YouTubes, Websites, inkscape.org

LXDE: Menu → Graphics → Inkscape
i3wm: ink - inkscape

PosteRazor – Image Enlarger

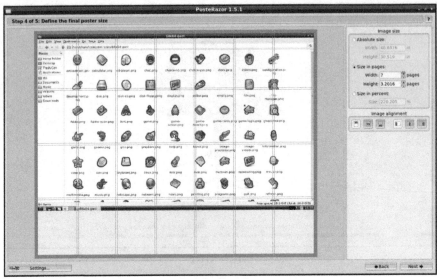

PosteRazor

Install: posterazor

Description: PosteRazor produces multi-page PDF en-largements of images. PosteRazor can accept BMP, GIF, ICO, JPG, PNG, TIFF, XPM, DDS, IFF, JBIG, JPEG, and most other formats.

Documentation: Click the question mark, top right.

LXDE: Menu → Graphics → PosteRazor
i3wm: po - PosteRazor

qpdfview – PDF Viewer

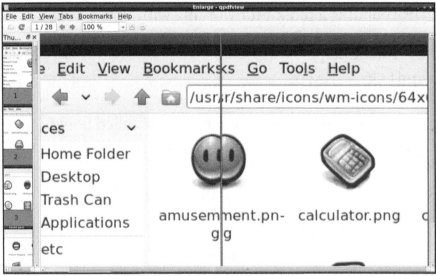

qpdfview shown with PosteRazor PDF output.

Install: qpdfview

Description: PDF Reader. Ctrl + A or Edit → Add annotation, select area, select Add text or Add highlight.

Documentation: Built-in help, man qpdfview
                        qpdfview --help

LXDE: Menu → Office → qpdfview
i3wm: qp – qpdfview

pdftk – PDF Toolkit

PDF Toolkit is a toolkit for working with PDFs.

PDF Tookit help:
```
pdftk --help
```

Assemble chapter PDFs to create a PDF called book:
```
pdftk ch1.pdf ch2.pdf output book.pdf
```

Split a PDF book int separate PDF pages:
```
pdftk book.pdf burst
```

ImageMagick

ImageMagick is a powerful bitmap processing tool. It can also be used for splitting and merging PDFs.

ImageMagick help:
```
convert --help
```

Assemble chapter PDFs to create a PDF called book:
```
convert -density 300 ch1.pdf ch2.pdf
book.pdf
```

Split a PDF book into PDF pages:
```
convert book.pdf page%03d.pdf
```

Qtikz – Diagram Editor

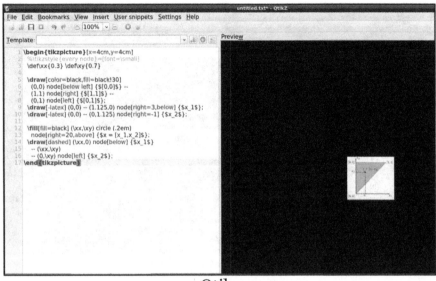

Qtikz

Install: qtikz

Description: Qtikz is a TikZ diagram editor.

Documentation: Help menu → Qtikz Handbook.
YouTubes, Websites
Search on "Tikz diagrams".

Examples: texample.net/tikz/
Examples: pgfplots.net

LXDE: Menu → Office → Qtikz
i3wm: qti - Qtiz

Magnus – Screen Utility

Magnus Screen Magnifier

Install: magnus
After installing: From a terminal:
```
sudo rm /etc/xdg/autostart/magnus*
```

Description: At startup Magnus opens a resizable magnification window which can scale the area around the mouse pointer by up to 5x.

Documentation: man magnus

LXDE: Menu → Utility Access → Magnus
i3wm: mag - magnus

Xpad – Notepad

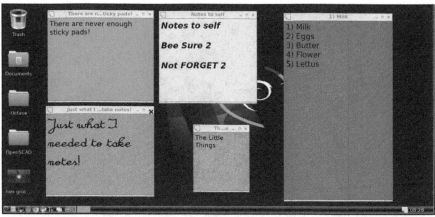

Xpad

Install: xpad

Description: Notepads, **Kanban method** may also be of interest. If the **Tray icon** fails to show, change the launch command to **xpad -t** and add it to the **Application Launch Bar** (Page 38) then uncheck **Enable tray icon**.

Documentation: Built-in help right click on an Xpad.
man xpad, xpad --help

Recommended Xpad Preferences

<u>**View tab - Check:**</u>
Show scrollbar
Show window decorations
Hide all notes from the taskbar and...
<u>**Layout tab - Select:**</u>
Use this font
Use these colors

<u>**Startup tab - Check:**</u>
Nothing checked
<u>**Tray tab - Check:**</u>
  Enable tray icon
  Tray left mouse click behavior:
    Toggle Show All
<u>**Other tab - Check:**</u>
  Confirm pad deletion

LXDE: Menu → Accessories → Xpad
i3wm: xp – xpad

Blender – Animation

Blender

Install: blender

Description: Create 2D and 3D animation. Blender has been used to create movies.

Documentation: Built-in Help, YouTubes, Websites, blender.org, Books

LXDE: Menu → Graphics → Blender
i3wm: bl - Blender

Synfig Studio – 2D Animation

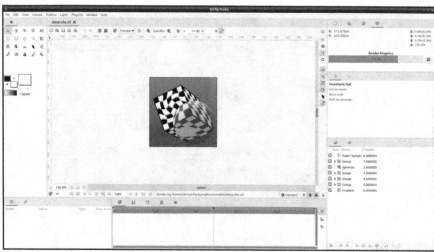

Synfig Studio – Rendering Warpcube Example

Install: synfig, synfigstudio, ffmpeg, ffmpegdoc

Description: Synfig Studio is a 2D animation studio.

Example:
Copy /usr/share/doc/synfig-examples to /home/userland
File → Close Document
File → Open **cells.sif** fast example, **warpcube.sif** slow.
For the **Warning**, click the **Close** button.
File → **Render**
Target pull-down select **ffmpeg**
Click the **Render** button.

Documentation: Built-in Help, YouTubes, synfig.org

LXDE: Menu → Graphics → Synfig Studio
i3wm: synf – Synfig Studio

Flowblade – Video Editor

Flowblade

Install: flowblade

Description: Flowblade is a video editor. A key feature of Flowblade is its use of rendering, which allows videos to be edited in low resolution and then rendered in high resolution.

Documentation: YouTube is the best way to learn Flowblade.

LXDE: Menu → Sound & Video → flowblade
i3wm: flo - flowblade

Media Conversion

FFmpeg - **Description:** FFmpeg is the leading multimedia framework, able to decode, encode, transcode, mux, demux, stream, filter and play pretty much anything that humans and machines have created. It supports the most obscure ancient formats up to the cutting edge.

Install: ffmpeg, ffmpeg-doc

Documentation: man ffmpeg, ffmpeg --help From PC-ManFM, right click on: /usr/share/doc/ffmgep/manual/ffmpeg.html and select Firefox. Websites and YouTubes dedicated to FFmpeg.

CLI: ffmpeg --help

ImageMagick - **Description:** A bitmap image composer and converter.

Install: imagemagick

Documentation: imagemagick.org/index.php
Websites, man convert, convert --help

CLI: convert --help

Kazam – Screen Recorder

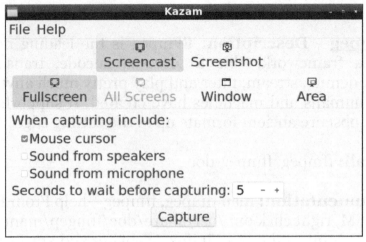

Kazam

Install: kazam

Description: Kazam is a screen recorder that can record fullscreen, windows, or areas. File → Preferences, to set preferences. Videos are saved in the users home directory in the **Videos** folder. To quit, left click on the tray icon and select **Quit** or **Finish Recording**.

Documentation: man kazam, kazam --help

LXDE: Menu → Sound & Video → Kazam
i3wm: ka - Kazam

vokoscreenNG – Screen Recorder

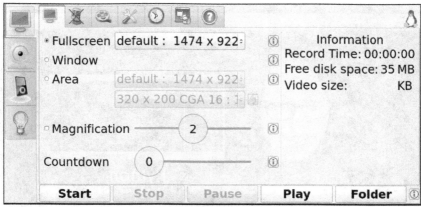

vokoscreenNG

Install: vokoscreen

Description: vokoscreenNG is a screen recorder that can record fullscreen, windows, or areas. Videos are saved in the users home directory in the **Videos** folder. To quit, right click on the tray icon and select **Exit**.

Documentation: man vokoscreenNG
vokoscreenNG --help

LXDE: Menu → Sound & Video → volkscreenNG
i3wm: vo - vokoscreenNG

MPV & SMPlayer

SMPlayer

Description: The MPV and SMPlayer install with LXDE.

Documentation: man mpv, mpv --help, mpv --list-options
man smplayer, --smplayer --help

MPV Shortcuts

F - Fullscreen
I - Information
L - Loop a-b, Shift + L - Loop entire video.
M - Mute
P - Pause / Play
Q - Quit
S - Screenshot - saves to home directory.
T - Move Subtitle
V - Display Subtitles
9 - Decrease Volume
0 - Increase Decrease Volume (Zero)
Spacebar - Pause / Play
Cursor Left / Right - Advance Back / Forward

LXDE: Menu→ Sound & Video → SMPlayer
i3wm: sm - SMPlayer

Audacious – Music Player

Audacious

Install: audacious

Description: Audacious media player, plays MP3, Ogg, ACC, ACC+, FLAC, ALAC, WMA, and WAVE formats.

Documentation: man audacious, audacious --help

Customization Example:
View → Visualizations → **Appearance** side tab
Interface: pull down select **Winamp Classic Interface**
Skin: select **Refugee**
Click the **Close** button.
Click on the Audacious Display.
Ctrl + D - Size Toggle
Click the icon in the top left corner for a menu.
Load files from the Playlist Editor "PL" on the display.

LXDE: Menu → Sound & Video → Audacious
i3wm: au - Audacious

Audacity – Audio Recording

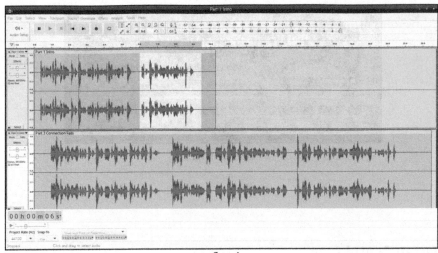

Audacity

Install: audacity

Description: Record, modify, and view audio files.

Documentation: man audacity, online help

LXDE: Menu → Sound & Video → Audacity
i3wm: audacit - Audacity

eSpeak – Speech

Install: espeak, espeak-ng, espeakedit

From a terminal: `sudo pcmanfm`
Copy files From: /usr/lib/x86_64-linux-gnu/espeak-data
           To: /home/<user-id>/espeak-data

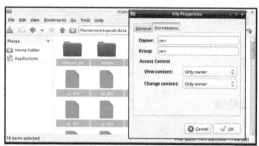

Change espeak-data permission.

Select all files (**Ctrl** + **A**) in /home/<user-id>/espeak-data
Right click on any file → Permissions tab
Change permissions to **Only owner**.

Documentation: man espeakedit, espeakedit -h
man espeak, espeak --help, man espeak-ng, espeak --help
           /usr/share/doc/espeak/docs/index.html
           /usr/share/doc/espeak-ng/docs/index.html
           /usr/share/doc/espeakedit/docs/index.html

From a terminal:
```
echo "would you like to play a game" > input.txt
speak-ng -f input.txt
speak-ng -f input.txt -w outputwave.wav
play outputwave.wav
speak-ng "yes I would"
```

LXDE: Menu → Sound & Video → espeakedit
i3wm: es – espeakedit
CLI: espeak --help, espeak-ng --help

DevedeNG – DVD Creation

DevedeNG

Install: devede

Description: Design DVDs which can be written to disk.

Documentation: man devede, built-in help,
/usr/share/doc/devedeng/html/select.html

LXDE: Menu → Sound & Video → DevedeNG
i3wm: dev - DevedeNG

Brasero – Optical Disk

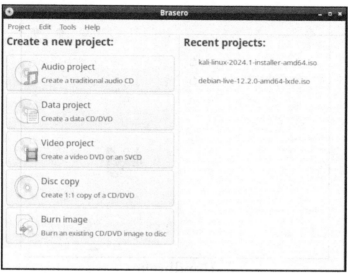

Brasero

Install: brasero

Description: Optical disk utility, read, write and copy
optical disks.

Documentation: man brasero, brasero --help,
built-in help

LXDE: Menu → Sound & Video → Brasero
i3wm: br - Brasero

Handbrake – Optical Disk

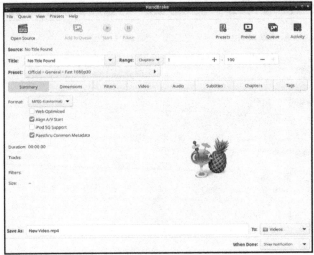

Handbrake

Install: handbrake, dvdbackup

Description: Optical disk utility, read, write and copy optical disks. dvdbackup can be used from the command line.

Documentation: man handbrake, handbrake --help-all
man dvdbackup, dvdbackup --help,

LXDE: Menu → Sound & Video → Handbrake
i3wm: ha – Handbrake

CLI: dvdbackup -i /dev/dvd -M

Ripper X – Optical Disk

Ripper X

Install: ripperx, cdparanoia, lame

Description: Optical disk utility, read, write and copy
optical disks. LAME and cdparanoia can
be used from the command line.

Documentation: man ripperx,
man cdparanoia, cdparanoia --help,
man lame, lame --help

LXDE: Menu → Sound & Video → Ripper X
i3wm: ri – Ripper X

CLI: mkdir ~/myMusic
cd ~/myMusic
cdparanoia -vsQ
cdparanoia -B
for FILE in 'ls' ; do lame $FILE ; done

LMMS – Music Studio

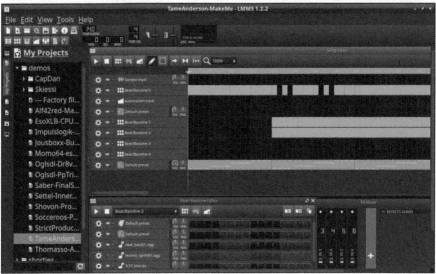

LMMS - Linux MultiMedia Studio

Install: lmms

Description: LMMS is complete music studio. Demo files are available in **My Projects** (left side icons), File → Export as **mp3**.

Documentation: Built-in Help online, lmms.io
YouTubes

LXDE: Menu → Sound & Video → LMMS
i3wm: l – LMMS

Mixxx – DJ Mixer

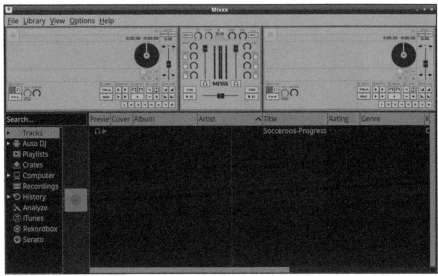

Mixxx

Install: mixxx

Description: Mixxx is a DJ Mixer that can be used for live broadcasting, or creating MP3s. It has support for MIDI devices and joysticks.

Documentation: Built-in Help online, YouTubes,
man mixxx, mixxx -help, mixxx.org

LXDE: Menu → Sound & Video → Mixxx
i3wm: mi – Mixxx

FreeCAD – CAD

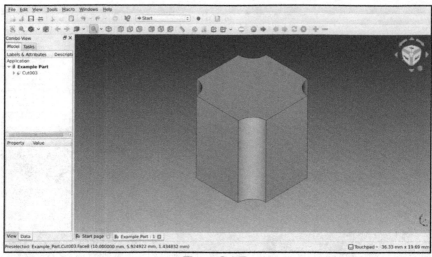

FreeCAD

Install: freecad

Description: FreeCAD is a full CAD system, which can be expanded with addons. FreeCAD is suitable for use with slicers and 3D printers.

Documentation: Built-In Help, YouTubes, Websites

LXDE: Menu → Graphics → FreeCAD
i3wm: fr – FreeCAD

OpenSCAD – CAD

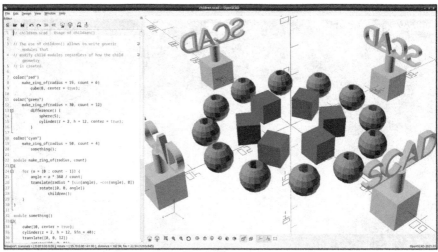

OpenSCAD   File → Examples

Install: openscad

Description: CAD that programs, interactive display.

Documentation: Built-in Help, YouTubes, Webpages,
Books, File → Examples.

LXDE: Menu → Graphics → OpenSCAD
i3wm: opens – openscad

UltiMaker Cura – 3D Printing Slicer

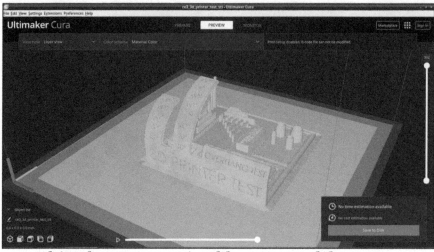

UltiMaker Cura – printables.com Model: 210803

Install: cura

After Installing: From a terminal:
```
pip3 install trimesh --break-system-packages
```

Description: Prepares 3D designs for printing by 3D printers. Cursor keys to rotate. Plus/Minus to Zoom In/Out. Hold Right mouse button while moving mouse to rotate image, hold Shift + Right mouse button while moving mouse to pan. Preferences → Configure Cura → Theme → Ultimaker Dark

Documentation: Built-in Help online, YouTubes, Webpages, man cura, cura --help, ultimaker.com

LXDE: Menu → Programming → Ultimaker Cura
i3wm: cur – Ultimaker Cura

Slic3r – 3D Printing Slicer

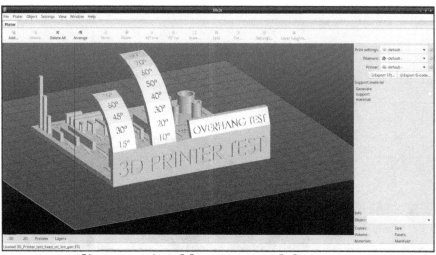

Slic3r – printables.com Model: 210803

Install: slic3r

Description: Prepares 3D designs for printing by 3D printers. Ctrl + Cursor Up/Down to zoom in/out. Hold Left mouse while moving mouse to rotate image. Hold Right mouse while moving mouse to pan.

Documentation: Built-in Help online, YouTubes, Webpages, man slic3r, slic3r --help slic3r.org

LXDE: Menu → Programming → Slic3r
i3wm: sl – Slic3r

Sweet Home 3D – Home CAD

Sweet Home 3D

Install: sweethome3d,
   sweethome3d-furniture,
   sweethome3d-furniture-editor,
   sweethome3d-furniture-nonfree, (See Page 272)
   sweethome3d-texture-editor

Description: Interactive 3D real-time home designer.
   3Dview → Ariel view (outside)
   3Dview → Virtual visit (inside)
   File → New from demo (includes demos)

Documentation: Built-in Help, YouTubes,
   sweethome3d.com

LXDE: Menu → Graphics → Sweet Home 3D (suite)
i3wm: sw – Sweet Home 3D

wxMaxima – Math CAD

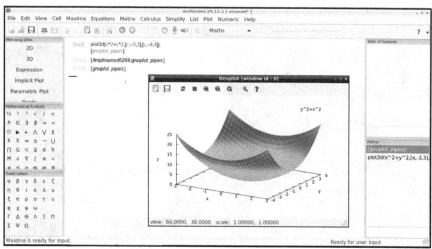

wxMaxima

Install: wxmaxima

Description: Math CAD

Documentation: Built-in Help, Websites, YouTubes

LXDE: Menu → Education → wxMaxima
i3wm: w - wxMaxima

Genius – Math CAD

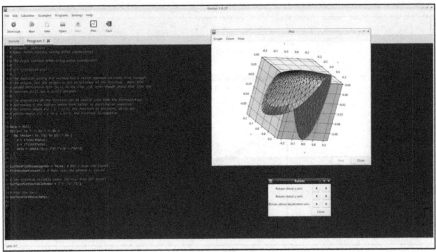

Genius

Install: gnome-genius

Description: Math CAD, highly intuitive design.
3D Zoom may crash program.

Documentation: Built-in Manual and Examples

LXDE: Menu → Education → Genius Math Tool
i3wm: geni – gnome-genius

Octave – Math CAD

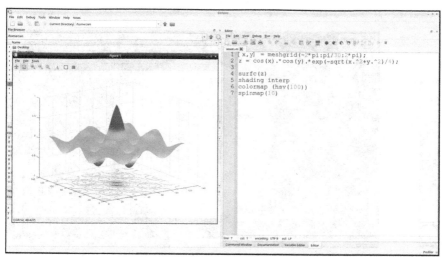

Octave

Install: octave, gnuplot

Description: Math CAD. Edit → Preferences allows
some font settings.

Documentation: Built-in Help, Websites, YouTubes.

LXDE: Menu → Education → Octave
i3wm: oct – GNU Octave

KDE Marble Globe – Science

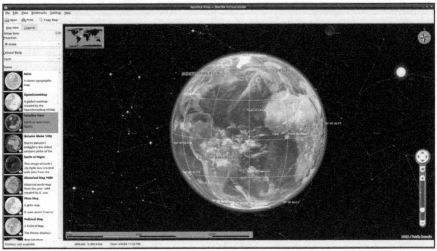

KDE Marble Globe Collection

Install: marble

Description: KDE Marble is a multi-purpose globe
collection. Maps can be zoomed down
to street maps or pulled out to the stars.

Documentation: Built-in Help

LXDE: Menu → Education → KDE Marble
i3wm: ma – KDE Marble

Kalzium Periodic Table – Science

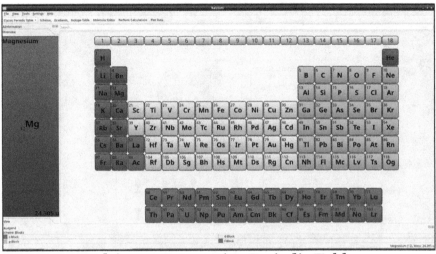

Kalzium – Interactive Periodic Table

Install: kalzium

Description: Kalzium is an interaction periodic table. At the time of this writing, the Molecular Editor is broken.

Documentation: Built-in Help, Webpages

LXDE: Menu → Education → Kalzium
i3wm: ka – Kalzium

Krita – Art Painting

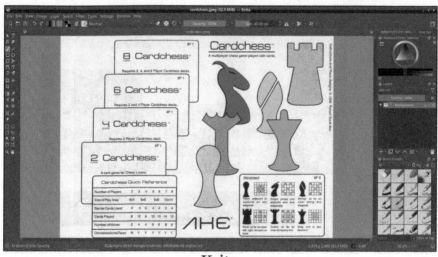

Krita

Install: krita

Description: Pixel based painting program.

Documentation: Built-in Help Online, krita --help

LXDE: Menu → Graphics → Krita
i3wm: kr – Krita

Mandelbulber – Art Math

Mandelbulber

Install: mandelbulber2 **Description:** Fractal Math Art
Documentation: Built-in Help. Websites and YouTubes.
File → **Load example...** → Click **Open** button → Click **Render** button top right. F11 - Toggle Image View

LXDE: Menu → Graphics → Mandelbulber v2
i3wm: mande – mandelbluber2

Onboard – On Screen Keyboard

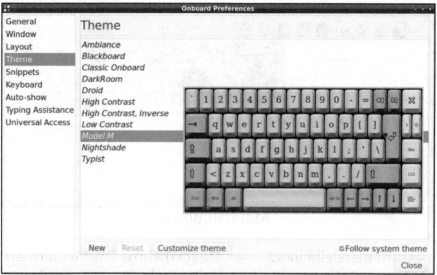

Onboard shown with Theme options.

Install: onboard

Description: Onboard is an on screen keyboard. Onboard has several themes, and layout styles. Second key down from top right is used to move the keyboard, which is resizable.

LXDE: Menu → Universal Access → Onboard
LXDE: Menu → Preferences → Onboard Settings
i3wm: on - Onboard / Onboard Settings

Screenkey – Keystroke Banner

Screenkey Banner

Install: screenkey

Description: Screenkey displays keystrokes in a banner format. Right click on the tray icon to set preferences; font, color, location, size and speed.

Documentation: man screenkey, screenkey --help

LXDE: Menu → Accessories → Screenkey
i3wm: scr - Screenkey

Figlet and Toilet – Text Banners

Figlet and Toilet Examples

Install: figlet, toilet, lolcat

Description: Create text banners from a terminal.

Documentation: man figlet, figlet --help,
man toilet, toilet --help,
man lolcat, lolcat --help

CLI: figlet --help, toilet --help,
lolcat --help

Xarchiver – File Archiver

Install: Installs with LXDE.

Description: Create, add and delete files from archives.

Documentation: Built-in help, man xarchiver

Create a new Archive:
Archive → **New**
Select a location and name the file.
Click the **Create** button.
Action → **Add**
Select files and or directories, click the **Add** button.
Archive → **Close**

Extract Files from an Archive:
Archive → **Open**
Select the archive and click the **Open** button.
Select files and or directories.
Action → **Extract**
Extract files panel, select options.
Click the **Extract** button.
Archive → **Close**

Open an Archive from PCManFM:
Right click on an archive.
Select Xarchiver.

LXDE: Menu → Accessories → Xarchiver
i3wm: xa – xarchiver

IDLE – Python

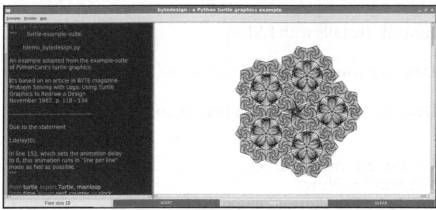

Python Help → Turtle Demo

Install: idle, python3-pip, python3-pipdeptree, python3-examples, python3-doc

Description: High demand, high paying area of programming, heavily used in AI.

Documentation: python.org, YouTubes, Websites, books, Help → Turtle Demo (Click **Examples**, select one and press **Start**.) Enter **file:///** into the Firefox or Chromium searchbar and navigate to **/usr/share/devhelp/books/python3.11/index.html** , bookmark.

Configure: Options → Configure IDLE, **Fonts** tab set fonts, **Highlights** tab set theme, **General** tab set **Auto-Squeeze Min Lines** set to 5000, click the **Ok** button.

LXDE: Menu → Programming → IDLE
i3wm: i - IDLE

Thonny – Python

Thonny Python

Install: thonny

Description: Thonny features a rich set of debugging options available thru the **View** and **Run** menus, which can greatly reduce the amount of time it takes to troubleshoot a program. Thonny's debugging features make it an ideal IDE for new programmers. There are many development environments for Python. Python files {dot} .py files are plain text files. Mousepad and Nano can also be used to write Python programs.

Configure: Tools → Options, Adjust scaling before selecting a font size. **General** tab, **UI Scaling factor**, **Theme and Fonts** tab, select themes and font size.

Documentation: Built-in Help, thonny.org

LXDE: Menu → Programming → Thonny
i3wm: tho - thonny

Custom Tkinter – Python

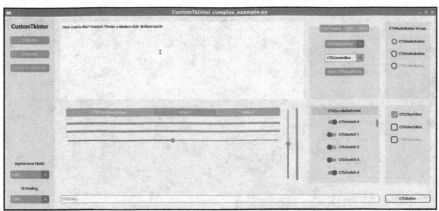

Custom Tkinter complex_example.py

Custom Tkinter by Tom Schimansky aka The Modern GUI for Python is a Python library that can be installed using PIP3.

To install Custom Tkinter
From a terminal:
    pip3 install customtkinter

Using **Chromium** download **complex_example.py**.
Go to the URL:
  github.com/TomSchimansky/CustomTkiniter
Open the **examples** folder.
Click **complex_example.py**
Click the **Raw** button.
Click inside the code area, Ctrl + A, Ctrl + C
Python IDLE → Ctrl + N, Ctrl + V
F5
Source Must Be Saved Ok to Save? Click **OK** button.
Pick a folder and name the program <name>**.py**
Click the **Save** button.

SQLite – Database

Note: Python is shipped with an SQLite library (import sqlite3). The R SQLite library can be loaded from Synpatic (r-cran-rsqlite) -OR- CRAN (install.packages("RSQLite")).

Install: sqlite3, sqlite3-doc

Description: SQLite is a serverless database that is implemented as a library. **sqlite3** is a text based SQLite query tool, {dot} help .help for help. {dot} .exit to quit.

Documentation: man sqlite3, sqlite3 --help, sqlite.org /usr/share/doc/sqlite3/index.html

CLI: sqlite3 - .help .exit

Install: sqlitebrowser

Description: DB Browser for SQLite is a GUI based SQLite browser editor.

Documentation: man sqlitebrowser
sqlitebrowser --help

LXDE: Menu → Accessories → DB Browser for SQLite
i3wm: db - DB Browser for SQLite

Command Line – R Language

The R Language is often used for big data analytics.

Create ~/.**Renviron**, from a terminal:
```
cd ~
nano .Renviron
  R_LIBS_USER="/usr/local/lib/R/site-library"
```
Ctrl + O, Enter, to save. Ctrl + X to exit

Install: gnuplot, r-base, r-cran-curl, r-cran-rgl,
       r-cran-multcomp, r-cran-sem, r-cran-leaps,
       r-cran-aplpack, r-cran-rcmdr

From a Terminal:
```
  R
  demo()
```
Cursor Up / Down, Q to quit.
```
  demo(graphics)
```
Ctrl + C to exit.
```
  help.start()
  q() to quit
```
Reply **n** to Save workspace ...

GNU Plot is a powerful plotting utility worth Googling.
```
ls /usr/bin/gnu*     Maybe gnuplot or gnuplot-qt.
man gunplot-qt       Use version listed.
gnuplot-qt
   set title "Trig Plots"
   set xrange [-6.28:6.28]
   set yrange [-2:2]
   set zeroaxis
   plot sin(x), cos(x), tan(x)
exit
```

R Commander – R Language

R Commander

Menu → Education → R Commander   (**Give it time.**)
or From XTerm, R, library(Rcmdr)

Set Font Sizes:
 Tools → Options... → **Fonts** tab
 Click the **Restart R Commander** button.
 Tools → **Save Rcmdr options...**
To Exit:
 File → Exit → **From Commander and R**
 Click the **OK** button. Click the **Save** button.

From the **R Script** tab enter the following, press the
Submit button at the end of each line:
```
letters
2 + 4  / 2
print("Hello World!")
```

Documentation: Built-in Help, Websites, YouTubes R
Commander is one of may GUI front-ends available for
the R Language.

Scratch – Programming

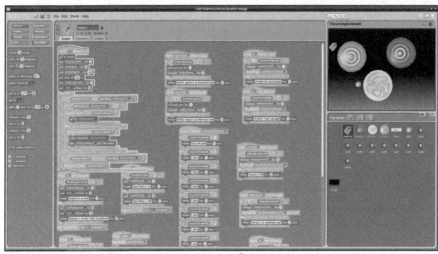

Scratch

Install: scratch

Description: Scratch is a Block Programming language created at MIT. Drag and drop programming.

Documentation: scatch.mit.edu, YouTubes. Also see:
developers.google.com/blockly

Example: File → Open → Examples → Simulations →
BouncingMusicBalls Click the **Green Flag**, top right.

LXDE: Menu → Education → Scratch
i3wm: scr - Scratch

Advanced BASH Scripting – Book

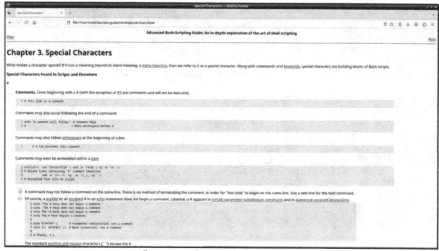

Advanced Bash-Scripting

Install: abs-guide

Description: To quote the book, "This tutorial assumes no previous knowledge of scripting or programming . . ." This is an HTML book that's read with a browser. Using PCManFM navigate to the index.html file and right click it then select a browser to open it with. Or, using a browser open the URL: file:/// and navigate to the index.html file.

While the shell language can be changed, BASH is the standard and there is a great deal of commonality between shells. BASH is basically unchanging, if it were to update weekly it would create havoc.

File: /usr/share/doc/abs-guide/html/index.html

htop – System

htop

Install: htop

Description: htop is process viewer. Left clicking a column title will rotate thru ascending, descending, and off. It can display opened and locked files. It can trace process system calls if **strace** is installed (Page 282). It can also kill a process, **F9**. And so much more . . .

Shift + Z – Toggle Pause Updates
Spacebar – Toggle Tag a Process

Documentation: man htop, htop --help, YouTubes

CLI: htop
    sudo journalctl -f   (View live logs, Page 239)

Disk Usage Analyzer – System

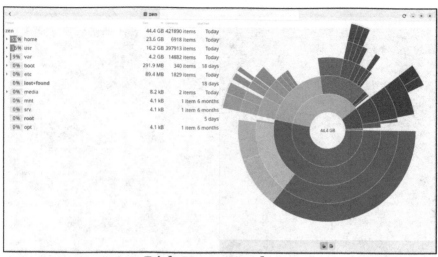

Disk Usage Analyzer

Install: baobab

Description: Disk Usage Analyzer is a graphical menu driven application for visualizing storage usage. Select a section by clicking form greater detail.

Documentation: man baobab, baobab --help

LXDE: Menu → System Tools → Disk Usage Analyzer
i3wm: disk - Disk Usage Analyzer

nInvaders – Games

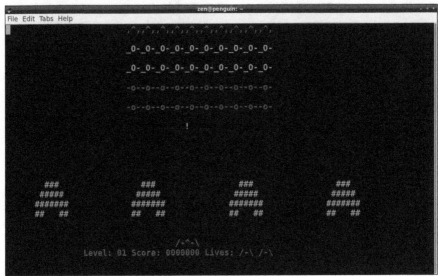

nInvaders

Install: ninvaders

Description: Terminal character arcade game. To enlarge the font size in LXTerminal: Ctrl + Shift + +. To reduce the font size: Ctrl + Shift + -. To permanently set the font size: Edit → Preferences → Style tab → Terminal font. **tint** is another fast paced terminal game.

P – Pause,   Q – Quit,   Spacebar – Fire,
Cursor Left / Right – Move Left / Right.

Documentation: man ninvaders, nInvaders --help

CLI: nInvaders   (Capital I - nInvaders)

Tint – Games

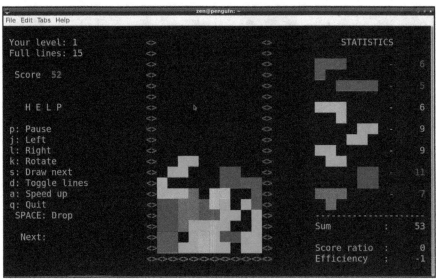

Tint

Install: tint

Description: Terminal character arcade game. To set LXTerminal fonts size, Edit → Preferences → Style tab → Terminal font. For level to start try 1.

> P – Pause,   Q – Quit, K – Rotate Piece
> Cursor Left / Right – Move Left / Right.

Documentation: man tint, tint --help
                                    See left side of screen for help.

CLI: tint

KPatience – Games

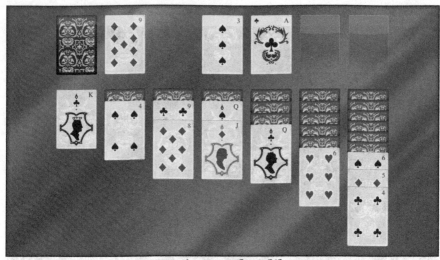

KPatience Klondike

Install: kpat

Description: KPatience plays 12 solitaire card games. Alt + F11 - Full Screen Toggle. Settings → uncheck Menubar, Toolbar, and Statusbar, to hidden them, Ctrl + M is the hide Menubar toggle.

Documentation: man kpat, kpat --help
             Help → KPatience Handbook

LXDE: Menu → Games → Kpatience
i3wm: k - KPatience

Gnome-Mahjongg – Games

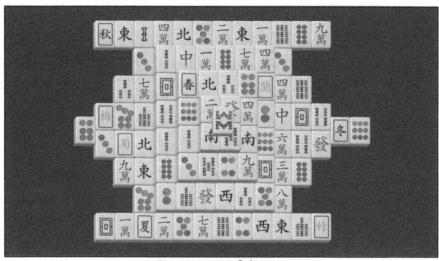

Gnome-Mahjongg

Install: gnome-mahjongg

Description: Solitary Mahjongg, includes 10 starting
layouts. Ctrl + H = Hint
Alt + F11 – Fullscreen, Ctrl + Q = Quit
Ctrl + ? = Show Keyboard Shortcuts
Ctrl + Z = Undo, Shift + Ctrl + Z = Redo

Documentation: man gnome-mahjongg, Menu

LXDE: Menu → Games → Mahjongg
i3wm: ma - Mahjongg

Neverputt Miniature Golf – Games

Neverputt Miniature Golf

Install: neverputt

Description: 3D Miniature Golf game for up to four players. Esc – Pause / Menu, Mouse Left/Right = Rotate Screen Left/Right, Mouse Forward/Back = Decrease/Increase force on ball, Left click = Release Ball.

Documentation: man neverputt, YouTubes

LXDE: Menu → Games → Neverputt
i3wm: ne - Neverputt

FooBillard++ – Games

FooBillard++

Install: foobillardplus

Description: 3D Billard game for one to two players. Alt + F11 – Full Screen. Esc for menu / quit.

Documentation: Built-in help, man foobillardplus
foobillardplus --help

LXDE: Menu → Games → FooBillard++
i3wm: fo - FooBillard++

Brutal Chess – Games

Brutal Chess

Install: brutalchess

Description: Left click a piece to select, Esc to release a piece, left click a destination square to place a piece. Right click and hold to move the board. Esc for menu, maybe missing letters, uit is Quit. Modifiy the launch command to set features, see **brutalchess --help** for options:
brutalchess -f -z 1400x1050
brutalchess -f -z 1400x1050 > keeplast.txt (Keep all: >>)

Documentation: man brutalchess, brutalchess --help

LXDE: Menu → Games → Brutal Chess
i3wm: bru – Brutal Chess

Kigo – Games

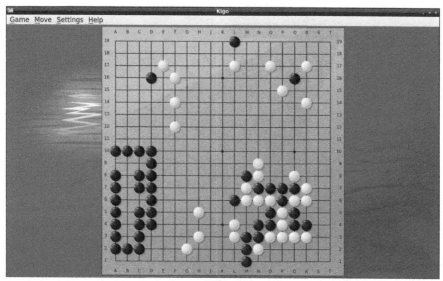

Kigo

Install: kigo

Description: Allows a choice of board sizes.

Documentation: kigo --help-all
Help → Kigo Handbook

LXDE: Menu → Games → Kigo
i3wm: ki - Kigo

Xiangqi – Games

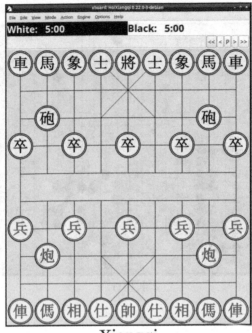

Xiangqi

Install: hoichess (installs hoixiangqi), xboard

Documentation: man xboard, xboard -- help
man hoixiangqi, hoixiangqi --help

CLI: Create a Go script, see Page 271:

```
xboard -fcp hoixiangqi \
-liteBackTextureFile /usr/share/games/\
xboard/themes/textures/xqboard-9x10.png \
-darkBackTextureFile /usr/share/games/\
xboard/themes/textures/xqboard-9x10.png \
-overrideLineGap 0 \
-pieceImageDirectory /usr/share/games/\
xboard/themes/xiangqi \
-trueColors true
```

Chess – Games

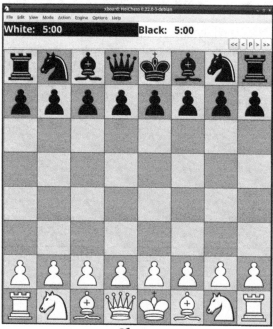

Chess

Install: hoichess, xboard

Documentation: man xboard, xboard -- help
man hoichess, hoichess --help

CLI: Create a Go script, see Page 271:

```
xboard -fcp hoichess \
-liteBackTextureFile /usr/share/games/\
xboard/themes/textures/wood_l.png \
-darkBackTextureFile /usr/share/games/\
xboard/themes/textures/wood_d.png \
-pieceImageDirectory /usr/share/games/\
xboard/themes/default \
-trueColors true
```

Shogi Variants – Games

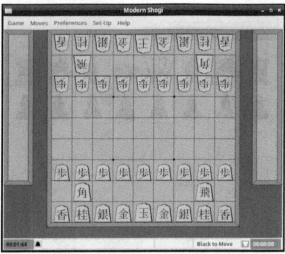

Shogi Variants - Modern

Install: shogivar

Description: Shogi Variants plays Modern Shogi and
many historical variants.
To exit: Game → Quit

Documentation: man shogivar, Built-in Help

LXDE: Menu → Debian → Games → Board → Shogi Variants
i3wm: sho – Shogi Variants

Xshogi – Games

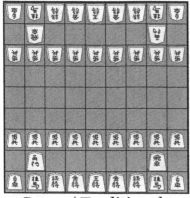
Green / Traditional

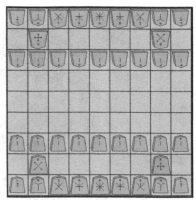
Blue / Arrow Icon

Example Configurations:
Green: xshogi -pc "#FFFFAA" -sc yellow4
Blue: xshogi -pc "#00AAFF" -sc gray -wps True

Install: xshogi

Description: See **xshogi --help** for options. Modify the launch command for various effects. Colors can be set using color names or hex codes. Page 52. To set foreground, background, screen size:
  -fg "#FFFFFF" -bg "#FF0000" -geometry "1920x1080"

Documentation: man xshogi, xshogi --help,
                           Built-in Help

LXDE: Menu → Games → Xshogi
i3wm: xsh – Xshogi

Flight of the Amazon Queen-Games

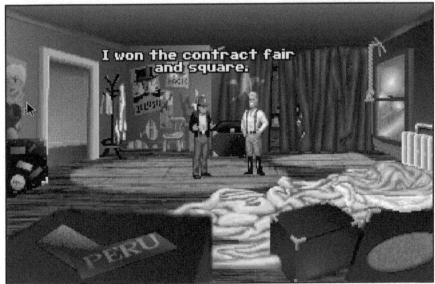

Flight of the Amazon Queen

Install: flight-of-the-amazon-queen

Description: Uses the Scumm VM backend. For more adventure games search on "scumm". Controls: Esc - skip intro, O - Open, C - Close, L - Look, P - Pickup, U - Use, F - Fast Mode. F5 - Game Menu (Esc return to game). Alt + F11 - Full Screen Toggle. (To start the game in full screen, edit the launch command, add a dash f, **-f** after /usr/games/scummvm).

Documentation: man scummvm, Websites

LXDE: Menu → Games → Flight of the Amazon Queen
i3wm: fl - Flight of the Amazon Queen

Beneath a Steel Sky – Games

Beneath a Steel Sky

Install: beneath-a-steel-sky

Description: Uses the Scumm VM backend. For more adventure games search on "scumm". Controls: Esc - skip intro, F5 - Menu, hover over keys for a hint. Move mouse to screen top for inventory, left click to move, right click for action. F5 - Game Menu (Esc return to game). Alt + F11 - Full Screen Toggle. (To start the game in full screen, edit the launch command, add a dash f, **-f** after /usr/games/scummvm).

Documentation: man scummvm, Websites

LXDE: Menu → Games → Beneath A Steel Sky
i3wm: b – Beneath A Steel Sky

Extreme Tux Racer – Games

Extreme Tux Racer

Install: extremetuxracer

Description: 3D downhill skiing game. Cursor key Left / Right to turn, Up to accelerate, Down to slow down, Spacebar to jump, P - pause, R to restart Esc to exit.

Documentation: Built-In Help

LXDE: Menu → Games → Extreme Tux Racer
i3wm: ex - Extreme Tux Racer

Frozen-Bubble – Games

Frozen Bubble

Install: frozen-bubble

Description: Puzzle shooting game. Cursor Left / Right, Up to shoot, Esc to quit.

Documentation: man frozen-bubble, frozen-bubble --help

LXDE: Menu → Games → Frozen-Bubble
i3wm: fro - Frozen-Bubble

SuperTux 2 – Games

SuperTux 2

Install: supertux

Description: 2D jump and run side scroller game. Screen settings are in the Options menu. Cursor Left / Right to move, Spacebar to jump, Esc to pause or quit. When starting, Spacebar or mouse to select.

Documentation: man supertux2, supertux2 --help

LXDE: Menu → Games → SuperTux 2
i3wm: su - SuperTux 2

SuperTuxKart – Games

SuperTuxKart

Install: supertuxkart

Description: 3D arcade racer. Cursor Left / Right to turn, Up to accelerate forward, Down for backwards, Spacebar to honk horn, Esc to pause or quit. Ignore "Your screen resolution is too low to run STK."

Documentation: man supertuxkart, supertuxkart --help

LXDE: Menu → Games → SuperTuxKart
i3wm: kar - SuperTuxKart

Powermanga – Games

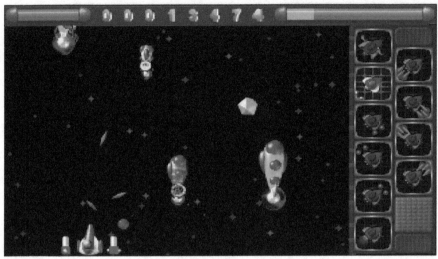

Powermanga

Install: powermanga

Description: 2D scrolling shooting game. The first time Powermanga is run press Esc then F – Fullscreen (Centers and enlarges the screen within the window.). Cursor keys to move, Spacebar to shoot, P to Pause, Esc to quit.

Documentation: man powermanga,
powermanga --help

LXDE: Menu → Games → Powermanga
i3wm: pow - Powermanga

GLtron – Games

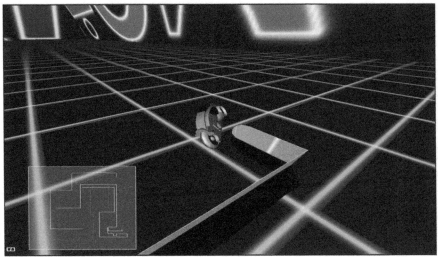

GLtron

Install: gltron

Description: GLtron is a tron-like 3D lightcycle game. Settings are available thru the menu. Use gltron --help to find the closest fit to the actual screen resolution without going over. For example for a 1920x1080 screen, change the launch command to: **gltron -6** (1280x1024). For fullscreen; edit **./gltronrc**, around line 35, change **settings.windowMode = 0**, from one to zero.

Documentation: man gltron, gltron --help

LXDE: Menu → Games → Gltron
i3wm: gl - GLtron

Battle for Wesnoth – Games

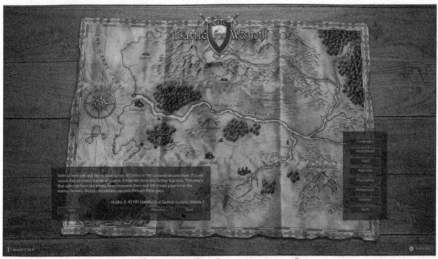

The Battle for Wesnoth

Install: wesnoth

Description: War game with an RPG flare. **Start with** the built-in **Tutorial**. The Tutorial is very detailed and a game onto itself. Tutorials can be found under Tutorial or Campaigns → Battle Training.

Documentation: man wesnoth, wesnoth --help
Built-in Tutorial, wesnoth.org
YouTubes, Webpages

LXDE: Menu → Games → Battle for Wesnoth
i3wm: we - wesnoth

Flare – Games

Flare

Install: flare

Description: 2D action role playing game. Cursor Left / Right to move, Spacebar - action, Esc - menu / back. Menu with shortcut list runs along the bottom of the screen.

Documentation: man flare, flare --help, flarerpg.org

LXDE: Menu → Games → Flare
i3wm: fl - flar

149

OpenTTD – Games

OpenTTD

Install: openttd

Description: Earn profits and win the game by building out transportation systems. YouTube is a good option for learning to play.

Documentation: man openttd, openttd --help,
openttd.org, YouTubes, Webpages

LXDE: Menu → Games → OpenTTD
i3wm: opent – openttd

Minetest – Games

Minetest

Install: minetest, (minetest* additional mods)

Description: 3D adventure block world game. Esc –
menu / quit. Key settings can be viewed and changed
from the menu. Alt + F11 – Fullscreen toggle. There are a
large number of additional modifications, mods, that can
be installed. Mod package names begin with minetest.

Documentation: man minetest, minetest --help,
minetest.net, YouTubes, Webpages

LXDE: Menu → Games → Minetest
i3wm: mi - Minetest

Torus Trooper – Games

Torus Trooper

Install: torus-trooper, cpulimit

Description: Torus Trooper is a short fast paced game. Esc - Menu / Exit. P - Pause, Z - Shoot, X (Hold then release.) - charge and shoot. Use cpulimit to slow down the game, 300% of 4 cpus = 3 cpus, 75 is 75% of one cpu, limit -l 75. Set **res** to the monitor size, 1920 x 1080 in the example below. Press X or Z to start.

Documentation: man torus-trooper, man cpulimit

Optional Go Script, /usr/bin/gotorus:
```
cpulimit -e torus-trooper -l 75 &
sleep 2
torus-trooper -fullscreen -res 1920 1080 &&
killall cpulimit
```

LXDE: Menu → Games → Torus Trooper
i3wm: tor – trous-trooper or gotorus

Trackballs – Games

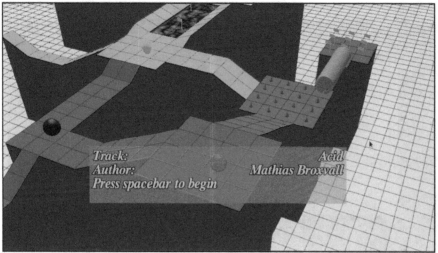

Trackballs – Marble Maze Game

Install: trackballs

Description: Maneuver a marble thru a maze. Built-in help
and game editor.

Documentation: man trackballs, trackballs --help
/user/share/doc/trackballs/trackballs/index.html
/trackballs.github.io

LXDE: Menu → Games → Trackballs
i3wm: tra - trackballs

Task Select – Software

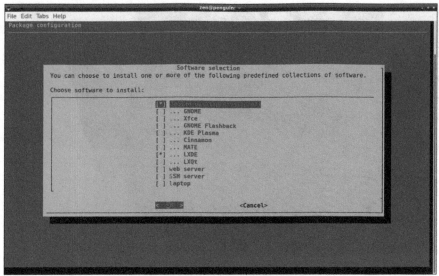

Task Select

Install: tasksel (and any desired "tasks")

Description: Task Select is a semi-GUI based software package installer that can be started from the command line. Search Synaptic for "tasksel", there are many "tasks" that can be added to tasksel to provide additional software selections. Software can be installed as a groups of related software.

Documentation: man tasksel

CLI: sudo tasksel

GDebi – Software

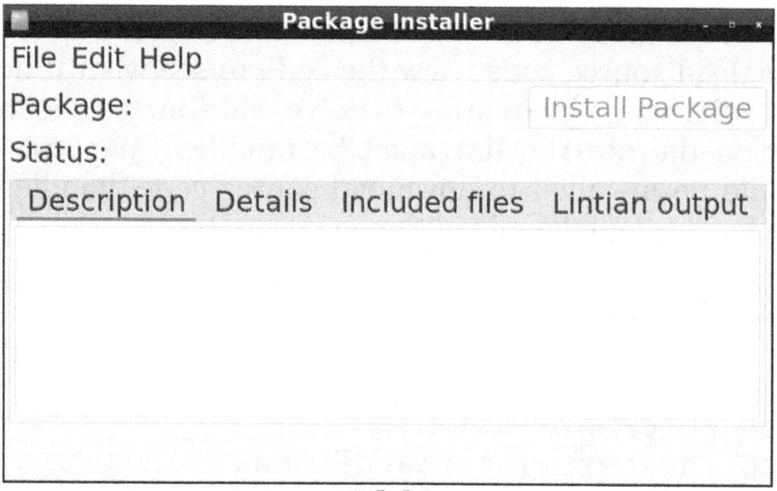

Package Installer	_ □ x
File Edit Help	
Package:	Install Package
Status:	

Description   Details   Included files   Lintian output

Gdebi

Install: gdebi

Description: Like apt, GDebi can be used to install local deb packages resolving and installing dependencies. Unlike apt, it can also resolve and install dependencies for remote (http and ftp) packages.

Documentation: man gdebi, gdebi --help

LXDE: Menu → System Tools → GDebi Package Installer
i3wm: g - Gdebi Package Installer

Building Programs from Source

One of the great freedoms of Open Source is the ability to download source code, view the code to see what it does, and edit that code. In order to download source code from Debian the **source.list** must be modified and **apt-src** should be installed to download source code, handle dependencies and download the necessary tools.

From LXTerminal:

```
sudo su
cd /etc/apt
cp sources.list sources.bak
nano sources.list
```

Duplicate every line in the file. Then change the beginning of the duplicate line from "deb" to "deb-src".

```
deb https . . .        (Original Line)
deb-src https . . .    (Duplicate Line)
```

Ctrl + O
Enter
Ctrl + X
```
exit
```

```
sudo apt update -y
sudo apt install apt-src -y
sudo apt-src update -y
```

Next build Galculator from source and change the Help, About screen to display "glaculator ROCKS!"
　　Menu → Accessories → Galculator

Building Galculator from Source

From LXTerminal:

```
cd ~
mkdir source
cd source
sudo apt-src install galculator
cd galculator-2.1.4          (Or current version.)
cd ui
sudo nano about.ui.in
```

About 10 lines down, find **program_name**. Change **>galculator<** to **>galculator ROCKS!<** Then save the file:

Ctrl + O
Enter
Ctrl + X

Build galculator from source. Remove the installed galculator. Install galculator from the **.deb** file created by the build, the full name is required for the install.

```
cd ~/source
sudo apt-src build galculator
sudo apt remove galculator -y
ls *.deb
sudo apt install ./galculator… … .deb -y
```

To remove the source code:

```
cd ~
sudo rm -r source
```

DOSBox Emulator – Retro

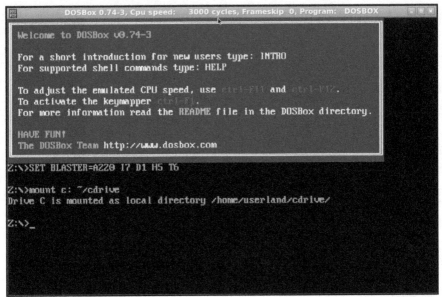

DOSBox Welcome Screen

DOSBox is an x86/DOS PC Emulator with sound and graphics support. It's popular with retro gamers and has many other uses. This allows any Debian Linux user to run x86 based assembler code.

As DOSBox has the advantage of a dead language in that DOS will never change, the environment is extremely stable. It is also universal, no matter what type of machine being used, if it runs Debian, it will work.

The Netwide Assembler, NASM, was designed to be cross-platform and is available thru Debian. In this chapter NASM and DOSBox will be used together to compile and run x86 assembler code.

Install: dosbox, nasm

Description: DOSBox simulates an x86 DOS PC. The cdrive directory acts as a virtual hard drive. Assembler code is written and then compiled by NASM on the Linux side. The assembler code should be compiled in or copied to the cdrive directory, where it can be run by DOSBox. The assembler programs can be written using any standard text editor such as Mousepad or Nano.

Documentation: man dosbox, dosbox.com, YouTubes
man nasm, nasm --help, nasm.us/doc

CLI: nasm --help

LXDE: Menu → Games → DOSBox Emulator.
i3wm: do – DOSBox Emulator

Run DOSBox once to create the configuration file in the ~/.dosbox directory. The configuration file should have a name similar to: dosbox-0.74-3.conf. If the file is deleted DOSBox will create a new one.

From LXTerminal:
```
cd ~
mkdir cdrive
cd ~/.dosbox
ls                          List the conf file.
nano dosbox-0.74.3.conf     Edit the conf file.
    At the bottom of the file add:
    mount c: ~/cdrive
Ctrl + O, Enter, Ctrl + X
```

In DOS, "**dir /w**" is the same as "**ls -a**" in Linux. The DOS "**dir**" is like "**ls -l**" in Linux. The DOS "**type**" can be used like "**cat**" in Linux to view text files. In the **~/cdrive** directory create the following three scripts:

```
d.bat
dir *.com /w
```

Make **d** and **m** executable.
```
chmod +x d, chmod +x m
```

```
d
#!/usr/bin/bash
ls *.asm
```

```
m
#!/usr/bin/bash

# Example to compile first.asm:  m first

if [ "$1" = "" ]; then
    echo "No file name"
else
    if [ ! e "$1".asm ]; then
        echo "File not found"
    else
        nasm -f bin "$1".asm -l "$1".lst -o "$1".com
    fi
fi
```

d and **m** are Linux BASH scripts, like scripts created previously in the /usr/bin directory. The **#!** sha-bang at the start of the file, tells the program loader what interpreter program to use. In this case it is not necessary, but it is a good practice. The **d.bat** script is a DOS script and must be located in the ~/cdrive directory. **$1** is the first value passed to a script. "**$1**" = "" is asking if there is a value, if not let the user know **No file name** was passed to the script. **! e "$1".asm** is asking if **<name>.asm** exists. **!**, not, **e**, exists "**$1**".asm, <name>.asm. It's a bit like talking backwards. If <name>.asm does not exist, tell the user **File not found**. NASM compiles x86 code text files into executable files that can be run by DOSBox.

It is rare that a master programmer like Oscar Toledo G. takes the time to write a detailed book sharing his insights. "Programming Boot Sector Games" by Oscar Toledo G. is one such book. He has written more, including "More Boot Sector Games". The books focus on x86 assembler code which runs on DOSBox. For Debian Linux users this means no matter what type of machine you have, Android phone or tablet, Chromebook, Raspberry Pi, or a computer you've built, the examples will work.

Using Firefox or Chromium go to Oscar's GitHub page:
github.com/nanochess
Click on **Invaders**
Click on **invaders.asm**
Click the **Raw** button.
Click inside the code area, Ctrl+ A, Ctrl + C
Open **Mousepad**.
Paste the program into Mousepad Ctrl + V
Around line 48, just under:
> **If not defined create a boot sector**
> Change: **equ 0** to **equ 1**
> Run as a COM, command not a boot sector.

Save the file as **invaders.asm** in the ~/**cdrive** directory.

From a terminal:
```
cd ~/cdrive
```

`d`	Will fail, not in search $PATH.
`./d`	Works **./** means this directory.
`bash d`	Will work, run **d** in BASH.
`echo $PATH`	Search path for executables.
`which d`	Returns nothing, not found.
`sudo mv d /usr/bin/`	**mv** is the move command.
`sudo mv m /usr/bin/`	Move can also rename files.
`which d`	Returns the path to d.

x86 assembler programs will likely be easier to write on the Linux side. The programs must be compiled by NASM on the Linux side. The .COM programs created by NASM must be run in DOSBox. In short, create it on Linux and run it on DOSBox.

It's convenient to have DOSBox on one virtual desktop and a Linux terminal on another and use Alt + Ctrl + cursor Left / Right to switch between them.

If files show up in Linux but not in DOSBox, in DOSBox press Ctrl + F4 to refresh the file list.

From DOSBox:

`intro`	Introduction, press any key.
`help`	Short command list.
`help /all`	Long command list.
`dir /?`	<command> /? short help
`dir`	Directory list with details.
`dir /w`	Just file names.
`dir /p`	Pause between screens.
`c:`	Switch to ~/cdrive.
`z:`	Switch back to z drive.
`type autoexec.bat`	View .bat file.
`exit`	Quit DOSBox.

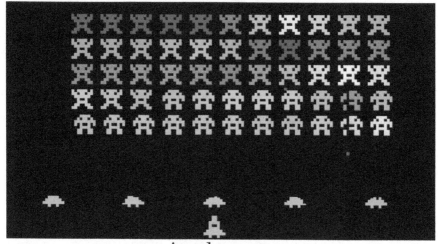

invaders.com

Controls: Ctrl = Move Left, Alt = Move Right
Shift = Shoot, Scroll Lock = Quit

From DOSBox:
```
c:
dir
```

From a Linux terminal:
```
cd ~/cdrive
```
Compile invaders.asm using the m script or nasm:
```
m invaders
```
                    -OR-
```
nasm -f bin invaders.asm -o invaders.com
```


From DOSBox, c: drive:

`dir`	invaders.com will not show.
Ctrl + F4	Refresh the file list.
`dir`	invaders.com is now visable.
`d`	d script displays only .COM files.
`invaders`	Run invaders.com.

S-100 Simulator – Retro

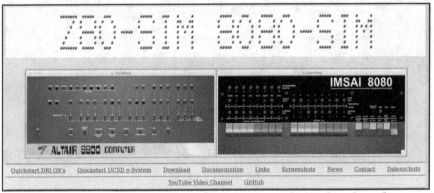

icl1900.co.uk/**unix4fun**/z80pack/index.html

The MITS Altair 8800 introduced in 1975 marked the birth of the home computer. It was built around the Intel 8080 the first general purpose microprocessor suitable for home computers. Soon after followed by the IMSAI 8080 which was featured in the 1983 movie WarGames.

Udo Munk stands out as a Computer Historian preserving the history and technology of home computers thru simulation. youtube.com/@udomunk github.com/udo-munk. From **unix4fun** download:

Do a find on 580, chess, 2.2 man, and super.

Disk image with Colossal Cave adventure, version B03, 580 points — Download

Disk image with CP/M Chess programs — Download

CP/M 2.2 manual set (PDF) — Download

Disk image with Microsoft Basic interpreters. Included are BASIC Rev. 4.51, BASIC-80 Rev. 5.21 and BASIC-85 Rev. 5.29. Also includes Super Startrek BASIC program adapted for ANSI terminals. — Download

From the CP/M 2.2 submenu select:
CPM Operating System...

UNIX host programs	
Z80/8080 CPU simulation, Z80 cross assembler, CP/M system simulation including boot disk images with CP/M 2.2, CP/M 3, MP/M 2 and a harddisk image with many CP/M tools, language compilers etc., simulations of the Altair, IMSAI and Cromemco systems	Download

Select the simulations just under Downloads, directly under **UNIX host programs**.

From the sub-menu select **z8opack-1.37.tgz** or the most current version.

libglu1-mesa-dev, libjpeg-dev,
From Synaptic install: **build-essential, libxmu-dev**

From **PCManFM** go to the **Downloads** folder:
Right **click** each **.tgz** file and select **Extract Here**.
Copy **z8opack** folder to **Home Folder.**
Rename the **z8opack** folder to **z80**.
In the **z80/cpmsim/disks** folder create the folder **backups**.
From the **Downloads** folder drill down into the **/disks/library** folder, select all the **.dsk** files and copy them to: **~/z80/cpmsim/disks/library**

From a Terminal:
```
cd ~/z80/cpmsim/disks/library
cp -p *.dsk ../backups
cd ~/z80/cpmsim/srcsim
make -f Makefile.linux
make -f Makefile.linux clean

cd ~/z80/cpmsim/srctools
nano Makefile
  #INSTALLDIR=${HOME}/bin          Comment out
  INSTALLDIR=/usr/local/bin        Uncomment
```
Ctrl + O, Enter, Ctrl + X
```
make
sudo make install
make clean
```

Under ~/z80/cpmsim/**disks**/ are two folders, **library** and **backups**, when downloading new **.dsk** files it is a good practice to place a copy in each.

Temporary **.dsk link files** are stored under **disks**. The CP/M Simulator is started with a **BASH** script. First it deletes the **old .dsk link files** that are linked to the **library,** then creates new ones and starts the simulator.

It will be necessary to edit a BASH startup script in order to access the downloaded .dsk files. **cpmsim** is a program and can not be edited. From a terminal:

```
cd ~/z80/cpmsim
cp cpm2 mycpm
nano mycpm
 #!/bin/bash
 rm -f disks/*.dsk
 ln disks/library/cmp2-1.dsk disks/drivea.dsk
 ln disks/library/chess.dsk disks/driveb.dsk
 ln disks/library/adv-b03.dsk disks/drivec.dsk
 ln disks/library/mbasic.dsk disks/drived.dsk
 ./cpmsim, $*
```

CP/M is an OS like ChromeOS.
If the simulator locks up, close
the terminal and restart it.
A:BYE to exit CP/M.

Ctrl + O, Enter, Ctrl + X

```
./mycpm
B:
A:STAT
DIR
MICRO80
60 50    →
```

WK is on 74

Moves WP.

R – Resign / Quit
N – No Board
D – Display Board

```
6 ! WP WP    WP WP ::    WP !
7 ! WR WN WB    WK    :: WR !
  +------ CHALLENGER -------+
MC : 33-44


      0  1  2  3  4  5  6  7
  +------ MICROCHESS -------+
0 ! BR BN BB :: BK :: BN BR !
1 ! BP BP BP BP :: BP BP BP !
2 !    ::    BB    ::    :: !
3 ! ::    ::    ::    ::    !
4 !    ::    :: BQ WP    :: !
5 ! :: WQ WP    :: WN :: WB !
6 ! WP WP    WP WP ::    WP !
7 ! WR WN WB    WK    :: WR !
  +------ CHALLENGER -------+

:  ■
```

```
                THE USS ENTERPRISE --- NCC-1701

                                            ,------*------,
                          ,-------------    '---  ------'
                          '--------- --'        / /
                            ,---' '-------/ /--,
                                 '--------------'

YOUR ORDERS ARE AS FOLLOWS:
---------------------------
    DESTROY THE 19 KLINGON WARSHIPS WHICH HAVE INVADED
    THE GALAXY BEFORE THEY CAN ATTACK FEDERATION HEADQUARTERS
    ON STARDATE 2428. THIS GIVES YOU 28 DAYS. THERE ARE
    3 STARBASES IN THE GALAXY FOR RESUPPLYING YOUR SHIP.

ARE YOU READY TO ACCEPT COMMAND ('N' FOR INSTRUCTIONS)? ▮
```

To exit, enter Y for instructions and 3 X's to quit.

```
D:
DIR
MBAS521
LOAD "STARTREK.BAS"
LIST
RUN

C:
DIR
ADV
```

BASIC – Beginner's All-Purpose Symbolic Instruction Code   (SYSTEM to exit.)

vintage-basic.net/games.html
thehighnibble.com
gotbasic.com

```
Welcome to the *new* Adventure!     Say "NEWS" to get up-to-date
game details.

Would you like instructions?Y

Somewhere nearby is Colossal Cave, where others have found fortunes in
treasure and gold, though it is rumored that some who enter are never
seen again.  Magic is said to work in the cave.  I will be your eyes
and hands.  Direct me with commands of 1 or 2 words.  I should warn
you that I look at only the first six letters of each word.
(Should you get stuck, type "HELP" for some general hints.  For info-
mation on how to end your adventure, etc., type "INFO".)
                              - - -



You are standing at the end of a road before a small brick building.
Around you is a forest.  A small stream flows out of the building and
down a gully.
>▮
```

Q – to quit.

S-100 Frontpanel – Retro

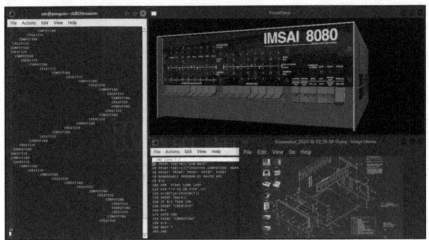

IMSAI 8080 Frontpanel

From a Terminal:
```
cd ~/z80/webfrontend/civetweb
  make
  chmod 755 libcivetweb.a
  sudo cp libcivetweb.a /usr/lib
  make clean
cd ~/z80/frontpanel
  make -f Makefile.linux
  chmod 755 libfrontpanel.so
  sudo cp libfrontpanel.so /usr/lib
  make -f Makefile.linux clean
cd ~/z80/imsaisim/srcsim
  make -f Makefile.linux
  make -f Makefile.linux clean
cd ~/z80/altairsim/srcsim
  make -f Makefile.linux
  make -f Makefile.linux clean
cd ~/z80/cromemcosim/srcsim
  make -f Makefile.linux
  make -f Makefile.linux clean
```

Altair 8800 Frontpanel

All simulators have start scripts and a disk library. If a simulator runs slow, don't start the desktop (gol), start the simulator directly from the ChromeOS Terminal. For both IMSAI and Cromemco click the power switch far right, then toggle the Run/Stop switch, two switches to the left, to Run. The Altair power button is on the far left, to it's right is the Run/Stop. If there are issues with the simulator, flip the power switch or close the window.

Cromemco Z-1 Frontpanel

VS Code – Program Editor

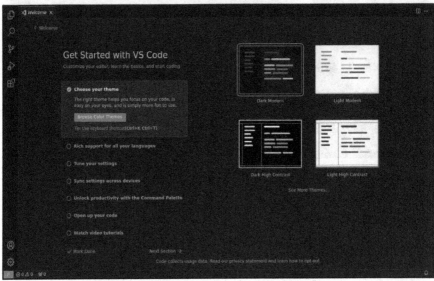

Microsoft Visual Studio Code Editor

Install: .deb file download

Description: To install the Microsoft Visual Studio Code Editor, the **.deb** file will be downloaded from the Visual Studio website and installed with **apt install**.

Documentation: code --help, Built-in, YouTubes, Websites

LXDE: Menu → Programming → Visual Studio Code
i3wm: Create a Go script.

code				
	barcode	0.99-4	Utility for barcode generation	
	catcodec	1.0.5-3	tool to decode/encode the sample catalogue for OpenTTD	
	cl-ppcre-unicode	20190407.(	Portable Perl-compatible regular expressions for Common Lisp (Unicode)	
	cl-unicode	20201101.(	portable Unicode library for Common Lisp	
	code	1.85.1-170	1.85.1-170	Code editing, Redefined.
	code-saturne	6.0.2-2	General purpose Computational Fluid Dynamics (CFD) software	
	code-saturne-bin	6.0.2-2	General purpose Computational Fluid Dynamics (CFD) software - binaries	
	code-saturne-data	6.0.2.2	General purpose Computational Fluid Dynamics (CFD) software - data	

Sections	**Code editing. Redefined.**
Status	Get Screenshot Get Changelog Visit Homepage
Origin	Visual Studio Code is a new choice of tool that combines the simplicity of
Custom Filters	a code editor with what developers need for the core edit-build-debug cycle.
Search Results	See https://code.visualstudio.com/docs/setup/linux for installation instructions and FAQ.

VS Code will show as **code** in apt and Synaptic.

VS Code – Install

Determine the Processor: Processors will either be Intel/AMD or ARM and have a size of 64 or 32 bits. Use the following 5 commands from a terminal:

```
arch                dpkg --print-architecture
uname -a            file /lib/systemd/systemd
getconf LONG_BIT
```

Download VS Code from: code.visualstudio.com

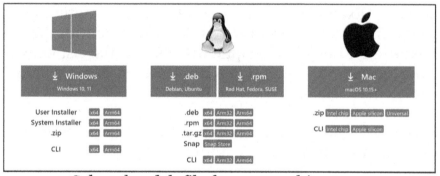

Select the .deb file for your architecture.

From a terminal (prefix the file with ./):
```
cd  ~/Downloads
ls *.deb
sudo apt install ./code… ...2158_amd64.deb
```

Watch for **code** after "will be installed:"
```
The following NEW packages will be installed:
  code
```

VS Code can be removed by using **sudo apt purge code -y** or from Synaptic with **Mark for Complete Removal**.

Software Best Practices

Doing a **sudo apt update -y** from time to time is necessary to keep APT working. Doing a **Reload** in Synaptic is also necessary to keep Synaptic working. If APT and or Synaptic fail to work, it may be necessary to do a **sudo apt update -y** and then a **sudo apt dist-upgrade -y**.

Look for built-in documentation. Most often a program will have a **man page** or **--help** option. Documentation for large programs may be located in a separate installer package (Example python3-doc). Look in Synaptic to see where files have been installed; Tool bar **Properties** → **Installed Files** tab. Synaptic will also list the last known Home page for the program. Configuration files may have comments in them.

Save work often while working. Use version numbers, myreport1.txt, myreport2.txt, myreport3.txt.

Test restoring a file, before it's necessary.

If a program fails try launching it from a terminal. Do an internet search on error messages. Check the program's documentation.

Check log files for error message (Page 239). In some cases strace may provide some insight (Page 282).

BASH scripts can be used to start and stop supporting programs or make configuration changes before and after a program is run, see Go Scripts Page 271.

TIDDLY WIKI

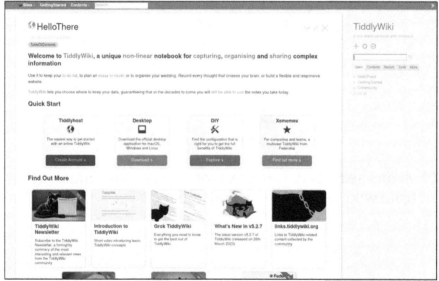

Tiddly Wiki Home Page

Tiddly Wiki is an eNotebook that runs on everything. It's great for school notes, recipes, photo albums, anything that might be done with a paper notebook. Go to **tiddly-wiki.com** At the top right:

Create Tiddler, Control Panel, Save Changes

Click on the **Plus Sign** icon under the Tiddly Wiki title. The Save Changes icon will change to a red circle.

Save Changes red circle icon.

Click on the **Save Changes** icon to save the Tiddly Wiki website wiki to the Downloads folder.

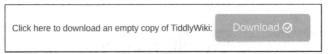

GettingStarted section Download button

Scroll down the page to the **GettingStarted** section and click the **Download** button to download an empty Tiddly Wiki to the Downloads folder.

Organizing Tiddly Wiki

In a move to protect users, operating systems in general and browsers often send files to a Download folder.

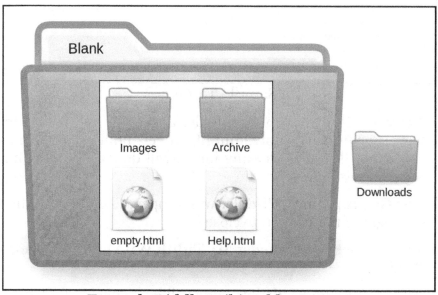

Example Tiddly Wiki Folder Layout

Create a folder named **Images** and another named **Archive** in a folder named **Blank**. Copy the two html files from the Download folder into the **Blank** folder. Rename the empty wiki file to **empty.html** and the other wiki file to **Help.html**. When starting a project copy and then rename the **Blank** folder and **empty.html** file to the project name.

At the end of an edit session, move the old wiki file to the **Archive** folder and prefix the name with the full date. Using YYYYMMDD will make the files easy to sort. Then copy the wiki (highest version number) from the Downloads folder to the project folder. Rename the file to remove any version numbers.

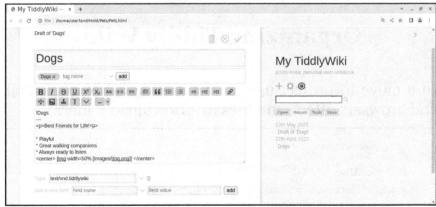

Sample Tiddler

- Copy the Blank Wiki project folder and rename the folder to Pets. Rename the empty.html file to Pets.html. Place an image in the Image folder any image will do. Open Pets.html with the a browser.

- The **GettingStarted** Tiddler will be open. Click the X at the top right of the Tiddler, to close it.

- Click the + Plus sign under **My TiddlyWiki** to create a new Tiddler.

- The default **New Tiddler** name will be highlighted. Change the name to **Dogs**.

- Just under the Tiddler name, enter a **tag name**. Enter **Dogs**, and press the **Add** button.

- At the bottom set the **Type** to **TiddlyWiki 5**.

In the **Type the text for this tiddler** section, enter the following. There is a space before **width** and after **50%**. There is a blank line after **</p>** use your image name in place of **dog.png**:

```
!Dogs
---
<p>Best Friends for Life!</p>

* Playful
* Great walking companions
* Always ready to listen
<center> [img width=50% [Images/dog.png]] </center>
```

Rendered Tiddler

Click the **Check Mark** at the top right of the Tiddler. The Tiddler will be rendered. Click the red Save changes icon to save the wiki to the download folder. Give the download a moment to finish, check the download progress before closing the wiki. Remember saves are sent to the Downloads folder.

Open the **Help.html** file in Chromium. On the right side, click on the **Contents** tab. Select **Working with TiddlyWiki**, this is a good place to start. Tiddly Wiki has been around since 2004 and even has an entry in Wikipedia. Googling Tiddly Wiki will produce pages of results. There are numerous YouTubes dedicated to Tiddly Wiki.

To change the color palette, click the **Control Panel** gear then select the **Appearance** tab and then the **Palette** tab.

Tiddly Wiki Page Breaks

Control Panel → Appearance tab → Theme tab

In order to use page breaks to control page layout when printing, the feature must be added to the theme's base Tiddler. Find the theme being used, click the **Control Panel** gear, then select the **Appearance** tab and the **Theme** tab under that. The theme shown here is the **Vanilla Basic theme**

Open	Recent	Tools	More

All	$:/Acknowledgements
Recent	$:/AdvancedSearch
Tags	$:/config/AnimationDuration
Missing	$:/config/AutoSave
Drafts	$:/config/BitmapEditor/Colour
	$:/config/BitmapEditor/ImageSizes
Orphans	$:/config/BitmapEditor/LineWidth
Types	$:/config/BitmapEditor/LineWidths
System	$:/config/BitmapEditor/Opacities
Shadows	$:/config/BitmapEditor/Opacity
Explorer	$:/config/DefaultMoreSidebarTab
Plugins	$:/config/DefaultSidebarTab
	$:/config/DownloadSaver/AutoSave

More top tab → **Shadows** side tab

```
$:/temp/search
$:/themes/tiddlywiki/snowwhite/base
$:/themes/tiddlywiki/vanilla/base
$:/themes/tiddlywiki/vanilla/metrics/bodyfontsize
```

Slide down to the theme's base Tiddler.

Click on the theme's base Tiddler and edit it.
$:/themes/tiddlywiki/<theme-name>/base

Add the following to the bottom of the file:

```
.page-break {
        page-break-after: always;
}
```

Add the following to a Tiddler to cause a page break:

```
@@.page-break
<p></p>
@@
```

Firefox Print Dialog Fix

The System Print Dialog does a better job than the Firefox Print Dialog. Open Firefox.

Enter **about:config** in the search bar.
Click the **Accept the Risk and Continue** button.
In the **Search preference name bar** enter:
    print.prefer
The **print.prefer_system_dialog** switch will display.
Click the **Toggle** to right, setting it to **true**.

Firefox Headers & Footers

Firefox headers and footers can be set from the Print Dialog or about:config settings.

Ctrl + P, Select the **Options** tab.
Select a value from the pull down.
If a value is already set to **Custom**, set it to **blank**, then back to **Custom**.

-OR-

Enter **about:config** in the search bar.
Click the **Accept the Risk and Continue** button.
In the **Search preference name bar** enter:
  print.print_head or **print.print_foot**

The values can be left blank, static text, or any of the following:
  &P (And Capital P) for Page number.
  &PT (And Capital PT) for Page with Total.
  &D (And Capital D) for Date and Time.
  &T (And Capital T) for Page Title.
  &U (And Capital U) for URL.

Defaults are:
  Top Left: Title
  Top Right: URL
  Bottom Left: Page # of #
  Bottom Right: Date/Time

Firefox Turn off Mouse Zoom

Enter **about:config** in the search bar. Click the **Accept the Risk and Continue** button. In the **Search preference name** bar enter: **mousewheel.with_control.action** Change the value from **3** to **0** (zero).

HTML Notepad

Bookmark the following link in Firefox or Chromium to create an instant notepad. Ctrl + S to save the notepad as an HTML file or Ctrl + P to print the notepad to a PDF. To edit a PDF note, open the PDF in a browser and copy the text back into the notepad. To edit an HTML file open the file in the browser. Bookmark **file:///** to add a file browser.

```
data:text/html,<html contenteditable="true">
<Title>Notepad</Title>
```

Browser Configuration

Browsers often have advanced features which do not have an obvious means of access. To access these settings enter the following in the search bar. In addition F12 will launch a Developer Options interface on all three browsers.

Firefox
```
about:about
```

Chrome
```
chrome://about
```

Edge
```
edge://about
```

SVG Graphics

AE World Model

	World Model		Explanation
Space	Object	Procedure	A World Model is the point of view through which the AE views
Attribute	Object	Group	the universe. Space is a place in which an Object can exist. An Object can perform a Procedure. Objects are defined by their
Step	Procedure	Event	Attributes and can be Grouped. Procedures can be divided into
Program	Life	Ecosystem	Steps. Procedures can be part of an Event. Life is a Program. Life requires an Ecosystem. A Thought is a Search. A Mind is a
Search	Thought	Mind	group of interrelated Thoughts.

In an AE a procedure is stored as a pathway, a series of nodes, it is a tangible object. When an AE node object is created, it's value is set to it's address and it is added to the appropriate groups. Procedures which generate other procedures will search for who, what, how, why, where and when. Affinities always provide the master why which starts a procedure. Procedures will be connected to objects, and have a beginning object state and an ending object state.

How do we get from a node to a mind?

 The answer is . . .

One pathway at a time.

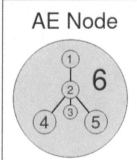

AE Node

1) Parent Node
2) Value
3) Drop Through Node
4) Left Sibling Node
5) Right Sibling Node
6) Address

AE Nodes are made up of six integers, which generally have a value between one billion and nine hundred and ninety nine trillion, 10 to 15 digits. The first billion nodes are reserved for special functions such as memory-mapped I/O, and character translation.

Tiddly Wiki page with SVG

SVG Scalable Vector Graphics are an XML-based vector image format used to create 2D images. Tiddly Wiki allows SVG graphics to be incorporated using the SVG tags.

SVG Example

```
<svg width="600" height="300">
  <rect cx="3" cy="3" width="594" height="294" fill="white"
  stroke="black" stroke-width="3" />
  <circle cx="120" cy="170" r="100" stroke="black"
  stroke-width="1" fill="rgb(210,210,210)" />
  <line x1="120" y1="97" x2="120" y2="187" stroke="black"
  stroke-width="2" />
  <line x1="120" y1="155" x2="160" y2="203" stroke="black"
  stroke-width="2" />
  <line x1="120" y1="155" x2="80" y2="203" stroke="black"
  stroke-width="2" />
  <circle cx="120" cy="103" r="15" stroke="black"
  stroke-width="1" fill="rgb(255,200,255)" />
  <circle cx="120" cy="155" r="15" stroke="black"
  stroke-width="1" fill="rgb(255,200,255)" />
  <circle cx="75" cy="210" r="20" stroke="black"
  stroke-width="1" fill="rgb(255,200,255)" />
  <circle cx="165" cy="210" r="20" stroke="black"
  stroke-width="1" fill="rgb(255,200,255)" />
  <circle cx="120" cy="193" r="12" stroke="black"
  stroke-width="1" fill="rgb(255,200,255)" />
  <text x="51" y="51" font-size="38">AE Node</text>
  <text x="113" y="110" font-size="20">1</text>
  <text x="114" y="162" font-size="20">2</text>
  <text x="115" y="200" font-size="18">3</text>
  <text x="66" y="221" font-size="30">4</text>
  <text x="156" y="221" font-size="30">5</text>
  <text x="157" y="155" font-size="50">6</text>
<foreignObject x="245" y="30" width="320" height="280"><body> 1)
Parent Node <br> 2) Value <br> 3) Drop Through Node <br> 4) Left Sib-
ling Node <br> 5) Right Sibling Node <br> 6) Address <br> <br> AE
Nodes are made up of six integers, which generally have a value between
one billion and nine hundred and ninety nine trillion, 10 to 15 digits. The
first billion nodes are reserved for special functions such as memory-
mapped I/O, and character translation.</body></foreignObject>
</svg>
```

SVG XML used to create the AE Node.

For more on SVG see the Help wiki, Page 175, search on SVG, see **Using SVG**. w3schools.com offers free lessons on SVG.

Tiddly Wiki Plugins

Plugins can be added to Tiddly Wiki to expand it's capabilities. To get started, click the Control Panel **gear** icon. The newly saved wiki replaces the current copy.

Click the **Control Panel** icon and select the **Plugins** tab. Then click the **Get more plugins** button.

Click the **open plugin library** button.

Click the plugin **Install** button.

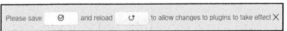

Click the **Save** button.

JUPYTER NOTEBOOK

Jupyter Notebooks are interactive browser based notebooks which utilize Python and markdown (md) text formatting. There are numerous addons and modifications available for Jupyter Notebooks. Visit jupyter.org to learn more. There are also numerous YouTubes on the subject.

If not already installed, from Synaptic install:

    idle
    python3-pip
    python3-pipdeptree
    python3-examples
    python3-doc
    jupyter
    python3-matplotlib
    python3-numpy
    python3-pandas

Jupyter Notebook Configuration

From LXTerminal:
```
cd ~
mkdir mynotebook
cd mynotebook
jupyter notebook --help
jupyter notebook --help-all
jupyter notebook --version
jupyter notebook --generate-config
```

Using Mousepad edit:
~/.jupyter/jupyter_notebook_config.py

```
Find: p.br
From: # c.NotebookApp.browser = ' '
  To: c.NotebookApp.browser = '/usr/bin/firefox'
```

Jupyter Notebook Markdown

There are numerous YouTubes on Markdown and many internet resources including:

markdownguide.org
wikipedia.org/wiki/markdown

Jupyter Notebook Example

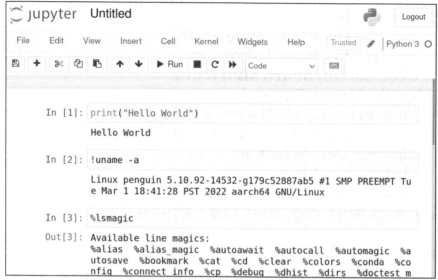

Jupyter Notebook

From LXTerminal:

```
cd ~/mynotebook
jupyter notebook
```

To the right under **Quit**, click on **New**, select **Python 3**.
A Python Notebook opens:

```
print("Hello World")
```

Press the **Run** button.

```
!uname -a
```

Press the **Run** button.

```
%lsmagic
```

Press the **Run** button.

Jupyter Notebook Help

Click on **Help**:
  Take the **User Interface Tour**.
  View the **Keyboard shortcuts**.
  Close the **Keyboard shortcuts**.
Select the **Home Page** tab.
  Click on the **box** to the left of the **ipynb** file.
  Click the **Red Trash Can** button.
  Click the **Delete** button.
  Click the **Quit** button.
  Close Firefox.
If servers don't stop, press Ctrl + C twice.

Firefox Font Size:
Ctrl + Shift + + Larger Font
Ctrl + Shift + - Smaller Font

Add R To Jupyter Notebooks

See R Language Page 122.

Add an R Kernel to Jupyter Notebooks.
From LXTerminal:
```
sudo R
install.packages('IRkernel')
IRkernel::installspec(user = FALSE)
q()
```
Reply **n** to Save workspace ...

GAMES

Games can stress a system more than most other application, particularly in the area of sound and graphics. Some misconfigurations may not be detectable until a system is under stress.

For example, playing Powermanga, tap F for fullscreen and audio stops working. The actual cause was misconfigured audio.

Resolving Fullscreen stops Audio.

- Take the app out of fullscreen.
- Close the app.
- Restart the sound server, from a terminal:
- `systemctl --user restart pulseaudio`
- Menu → Sound & Video → PulseAudio Volume ...
- From the Configuration tab, try a new **Profile**.
- Repeat as needed.

The **PulseAudio Volume Control** app can be started by right clicking on taskbar speaker and selecting Launch Mixer, from the Menu → Sound & Video → PulseAudio Volume Control, or command-line: `pavucontrol`.

PulseAudio Configuration tab

Testing PulseAudio Configuration Profiles will not harm anything. For sound issues close the app then restart the sound server, from a terminal:

```
systemctl --user restart pulseaudio
```
Then try the next Profile.

The ALSA speaker-test is a quick way to perform an audio test if. Install **alsa-utils**. From a terminal:

```
speaker-test
```

Display Settings

Misconfigured game display settings can cause fullscreen issues. Generally it is a good practice for a game's internal settings to match the actual display settings. This is another issue that may not show itself until going fullscreen.

Menu → Preferences → Monitor Settings

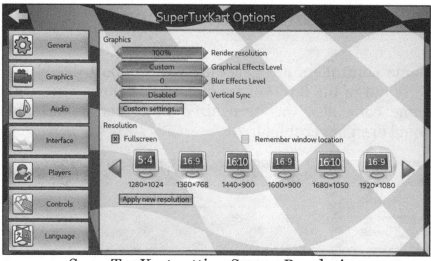

SuperTuxKart setting Screen Resolution

Quick Reference:
    Menu → Preferences → Monitor Settings
    Menu → Sound & Video → PulseAudio Volume Control

```
systemctl --user restart pulseaudio
speaker-test
```

SuperTuxKart in Fullscreen

Game Controllers

Game controllers are generally well supported and will work out of the box. For example the Logitech F310 USB game controller was recognized by SuperTuxKart and could even be reconfigured.

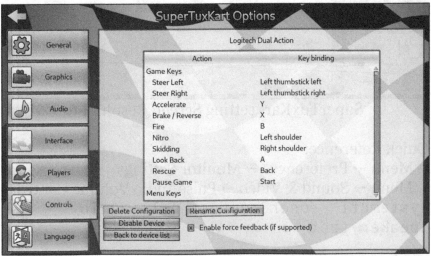

SuperTuxKart Game Controller Configuration

AntiMicroX

There are programs such as AntiMicroX that can add game controllers to keyboard based games. This can have application far beyond games and can be used with any keyboard based program.

Menu→ Accessories → AntiMicroX

Install: antimicro

Documentation: man antimicrox, antimicrox --help

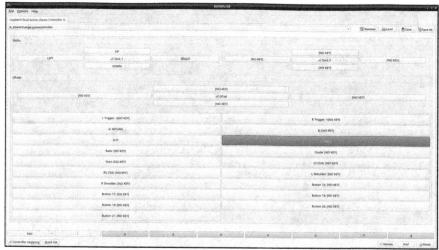

Menu → Accessories → AntiMicroX

AntiMicroX will display a game controller map of the connected controller. Pressing a controller button highlights the button on the map. Clicking that location on the controller map opens a keyboard map. Keys can be selected from the map or by pressing them on a physical keyboard. Key combinations such as Ctrl + L can also be used.

AntiMicroX Keyboardmap

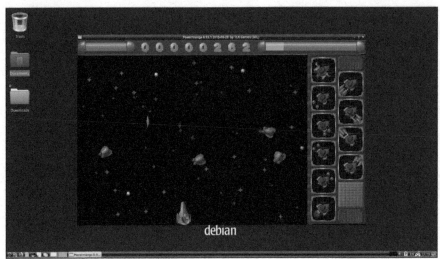

Powermanga using AntiMicroX

AntiMicroX allows the creation of profiles. A script can be used to start AntiMicroX with a profile for a specific game and then start the desired game. For the example below, the launch command would be changed to gopower.

Script to start and stop AntiMicroX with Powermanga:

```
sudo su
cd /usr/bin
nano gopower
   antimicrox \
     --profile js-powermanga.gamecontroler \
     --hidden &
   powermanga &&
   killall antimicrox
Ctrl + O, Enter, Ctrl + X
chmod +x gopower
```

Debian Game Controller Wiki Page:
  wiki.debian.org/Gamepad

PRINT & SCAN

Printer and scanner setup is automatic, while allowing for manual setup and configuration. The CUPS printer interface is accessed thru a browser. Xsane can scan multipage documents, and allows detailed control over quality and type of scan. PC and Scanner / Printer should all be on the same network. From Synpatic, install:

```
cups
printer-driver-cups-pdf
```

Verify the user-id with **whoami**. **groups** displays the groups a user belongs to. Then add the user-id to the printer management group with **usermod**. From a terminal:

```
whoami
groups
sudo usermod -aG lpadmin <user-id>
```

Shutdown and restart Linux to pickup the change. See also **Managing Groups** Page 265.

Printing with CUPS

CUPS Print Test Page

Open Firefox then go to and bookmark the URL:
`127.0.0.1:631 aka localhost:631`

Printers can be manually added here. Printers can be suspended and restarted. Output can be rerouted. Printer defaults can be set here. CUPS opens on the **Home** page tab. Click the **Printer** tab. Click on the printer name. From the **Maintenance** pull-down, select **Print Test Page**. To set the Default Options: Printers → Select Printer - Administration pull-down → Set Default Options. For **PDF**: Menu – Preferences → Printer Settings → double click the PDF printer → Printer Options.

Scanning with Xsane

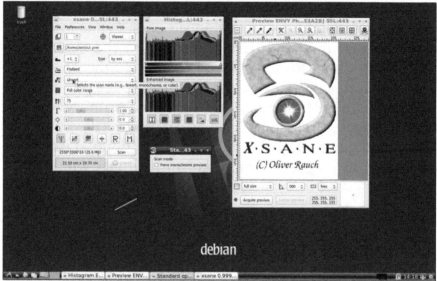

Xsane at startup.

Start Xsane:

> LXDE menu → Graphics → Xsane

Xsane will open four windows when it starts, only two are needed. From the primary window's **Window** menu, uncheck **Show histogram** and **Show standard options**.

Hovering over an option provides a pop up that describes the option. Some likely option settings changes are: Scan Mode from **lineart** to **color** and Scan Resolution from **75** to **300**.

Pressing the **Acquire preview** button will scan and display a preview. The entire image or any part can be selected for the scan. Pressing the **Scan** button scans the image which then opens in a Viewer Window where the file can be saved.

Multi-page scans are a two step process. Scans are saved as individual files and then appended to the desired file type when done. Press Ctrl + M or change the Target option to Multi-page (top right), the multi-page project window opens. Press the **Scan** button in the primary window to add pages. Press the **Save multipage file** button in the multi-page project window when done. Leave the **Number of pages to scan** set to 1 (primary window top left).

Embedded Web Server

Printers which use Internet Printing Protocol (IPP) often have an Embedded Web Server (EWS). A printer may not be using IPP or have an EWS. If it does, it can be a useful feature.

From LXTerminal:
```
ippfind
```

If the **ippfind** command returns something like: ipp:// **HP0068EBCE3A2B.local**:631/ipp/print copy (Ctrl + Shift + C) everything between **ipp://** and **:631**, for this example: HP0068EBCE3A2B.local Paste this into your browser's search bar.

BASH

There are two primary styles of interfaces; GUI, Graphic User Interface and CLI, Command Line Interface. For some tasks a CLI is the only way a task can be performed. CLI is also faster for some tasks. Generally entering a wrong command is unlikely to do much damage. Usually a misspelled command wont do anything. The Command Line empowers, it gives you control and access. **script** can used to record a **BASH** session, Ctrl + D to stop. **man script** and **script --help** for more information.

which shows what will run. **type** shows all programs with the same name in **$PATH**. **file** shows the kind of file. **stat** shows file details. From a terminal:

```
echo $PATH
which firefox
type firefox
ls -l /usr/bin/firefox
file /usr/bin/firefox
stat /usr/bin/firefox
cat /usr/bin/firefox
```

For more on BASH see Page 125.

```
which bash
man bash
```
Q
```
sudo su
    Tab Tab
    Y
```
  Hold down Enter or Q to Quit.
```
exit
```

echo prints to a terminal. > sends output to a file. >> appends output to a file. **$HOME** is a variable that holds the user's home directory. ~ is short for **$HOME**. **rm** removes, deletes a file. **cp** copies a file. **mv** moves or renames a file.

```
echo "neofetch"
echo "neofetch" > test.sh
echo "screenfetch" >> test.sh
cat test.sh
bash test.sh
./test.sh              Will fail.
chmod +x test.sh       Make executable.
./test.sh              Will work.
pwd
echo $HOME
echo ~
~/test.sh
ls
cp test.sh test2.sh
ls
mv test.sh test2.sh
rm test2.sh
ls
```

```
cat > test.txt
Line 1
Line 2
Ctrl + D
cat test.txt
cat >> test.txt
Line 3
Line 4
Ctrl + D
cat text.txt
```

Directories

Directories also called folders provide a hierarchical structure for organizing files. The **cd,** change directory, command is used to move between directories. **cd ..** is used to move up a directory structure. **mkdir** is used to make a directory. Use single or double quotes when a directory name contains a space. **rm -r** will remove a directory and any files or directories in it. **touch** will create an empty file.

```
mkdir numbers
ls
cd numbers
touch one
touch "two three"
ls
cd ..
ls
rm -r numbers
ls
```

Linux Process

Everything that runs on Linux is called a process. <id> is the process id. Htop can be used to kill a process, Cursor F9, Enter. From a terminal:

galculator &	Shows **\<id>**
pidof galculator	Shows **\<id>**
kill **\<id>**	Cancel using **\<id>**
galculator &	Shows **\<id>**
ps **\<id>**	Shows process **\<name>**
pkill galculator	Cancel using **\<name>**
ps -ely	Display all processes.
pstree	Display process tree.
galculator &	Shows **\<id>**
killall galculator	Cancel all processes **\<named>**
htop	System monitor, Q to Quit.

List Files Long Display

From a terminal: File type and permission:

```
cd ~              |    -rwxrwxrwx    r-read
ls                |    TUUUGGGEEE    w-write
ls -l             |                  x-execute
ls -la            |
ls -la | less     |    UUU - user         rwx
Q                 |    GGG - group        rwx
ls --help         |    EEE - everyone rwx
man ls            |    T   - type of file
Q                 |        - file
info ls           |        d directory
Q                 |        l link
```

202

I3WM ICEWM & TWM

The appearance, ease of use, efficiency, features, and methods of operations can vary greatly between Window Mangers. **i3wm**, **IceWM,** and **TWM** are three mature, light weight, small form factor **Window Managers** that play well with **LXDE**. Changing Window Managers changes how things are done, not what can be done.

As always it is a good practice to test new software on a test chip before installing on a primary chip or primary storage. Always **backup** a primary system **before installing** new software.

Until now the LightDM Display Manager has operated in the background, essentially invisible. The LightDM **Display Manger** manages **Window Managers** and is the primary method used to switch between Window Managers. It adds a step to the startup and shutdown.

When apps fail to launch from a menu, use a terminal:
```
sudo synaptic
connman-gtk --no-icon
gnome-screenshot -i
```
Closing the terminal will close the app.

Configure LightDM

Configure LightDM (Display Manger) for multi-Desktops, by commenting out all the settings, lines that are not sections titles. To comment out a line, place a # at the beginning of the line. Section titles are short lines enclosed in square brackets. Nano uses color highlighting which eases the process. From a terminal:

```
sudo su
cd /etc/lightdm
cp lightdm.conf lightdm.bak
nano lightdm.conf
    Comment out all settings.
Ctrl + O, Enter, Ctrl + X
```

LightDM Unable to Login

If LightDM loops and does not allow you to logon, commenting out LightDM special settings above and removing Xauthority files below will likely resolve the issues. For **Forgotten PC Password Reset** see Page 28.

Alt + Ctrl + F6   Open a Console.
Press Enter as need to get a prompt.
Enter **id** and **password**.

```
ls .Xauthor*
```
List Xauthor* files.
```
rm .Xauthor*
```
Delete files.
Alt + Ctrl + Del   Reboot

LightDM logs:
```
/var/log/lightdm
```

i3wm

i3wm is a manual Tiling Window Manager, which works by cutting a window into tiles, leaving no unused space. Manual, meaning the window tile to be cut and whether it is to be cut vertically or horizontally has not been preset. i3wm also uses Workspaces aka Virtual Desktops. Like most Tiling Window Mangers, i3wm is dependent on shortcut keys, which makes the i3 Reference Card a must have.

Tiling Window Mangers are known for their extreme efficiency. They are generally configured by editing a small handful of text files. i3wm has only one configuration file: ~/.config/i3/config. There is an excellent presentation on Tiling Window Managers by Aline Abler for Linux Days on YouTube. The **i3 Reference Card** is about half a page long.

Install: i3

The **i3wm.org** website is well organized. It's handy to download the **i3 reference card** and **User's Guide**, which can be found under **Docs**, by printing them to PDF. Video tutorials can be found under **Screens**. Alex Booker has an excellent series of YouTubes on i3wm.

Reboot

After installing **i3**, reboot. Select i3 from the pull down menu at the top right of the LightDM Greeter screen. Enter a user id and password.

i3wm First Run

The first time i3wm is run, it will ask two questions and generate a configuration file. Accept the defaults, press Enter for both questions.

Do you want me to generate a config file... :
    Press Enter for Yes.

Please choose either: Leave "Win" selected. :
    Press Enter to write the config.

This will create **~/.config/i3/config**, which can be edited or deleted without harming i3. If it is deleted the start up questions will have to be answered again. Press Shift + Win + E and click the **Exit** button at the top right of the screen to **exit i3wm**. From the **LightDM Greeter** screen, the system can be **shutdown** from the drop down menu at the far top right of the screen.

Shortcut Keys aka **Hot Keys**, are also configured in i3/config. **$mod** is set to mod4 the Win key, **mod1** is the Alt key. The **xmodmap**, **xev**, **sudo dumpkeys -l**, and **sudo showkey -a** commands are helpful for finding key codes. Be sure to download the **i3 reference card.**

Study LXDE launch commands, experiment, don't over think things, use the Workspaces. Launch Synaptic from a terminal; **sudo synaptic** then Win + W or Win + F. It's ok to exit Connman once a connection has been made.

Win + D conn → Enter	Select connman-gtk
Win + (0 – 9)	Select a Workspace.
Win + Shift + (0 – 9)	Move a Window.

i3/config

Add the following to the bottom of **~/.config/i3/config**. **xset q** displays screen settings, **xset s off** turns off the screensaver, and **xset -dpms** turns off power screensaver. As this must be done every time i3wm is started, it is placed at the end of the config file. From a terminal:

```
xset q
xset s off
xset -dpms
xset q
cd ~/.config/i3
cp config config.bak

nano config
```

In the key binding (bindsym) section add:
```
# Print Screen Key - Take a screenshot.
bindsym Print exec gnome-screenshot -i
```

At the bottom of the file add:
```
xset s off
xset -dpms
exec xrdb -merge ~/.Xresources && xterm
```
Ctrl + O, Enter, Ctrl + X

For a cleaner menu list change:
```
From: --no-startup-id dmenu_run
To:   --no-startup-id i3-dmenu-desktop
```

i3wm Floating Window

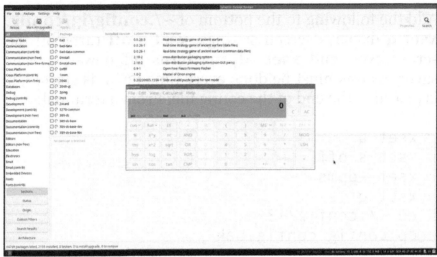

i3wm does allow Windows to Float.

Floating Windows:

```
sudo synaptic
```
Win + W
Win + D
```
galc
```
Enter
Win + Shift + Spacebar

Quit Programs:

Ctrl + Q
Ctrl + Q

i3wm Split Windows

i3wm Split Windows Format

Split Windows:

htop
Win + Enter
neofetch
Win + V
Win + Enter
cmatrix   I know right!

Quit Programs:

Q
exit
exit
Q
exit

IceWM Window Manager

IceWM - Menu → Settings → Themes → NanoBlue

Install: icewm

Description: IceWM is a nimble, very lightweight, quick to install, continuously updated, well documented Window Manager. It is configured by editing text files and does not offer desktop icons. More themes available at box-look.org, search on icewm. Start synaptic from a terminal: **sudo synaptic**

Documentation: /usr/share/doc/icewm/html/icewm.html
Built-in Help, ice-wm.org, YouTubes

Copy the files and folders   **From:** /usr/share/icewm/
Only edit files in ~/.icewm/   **To:** ~/.icewm/

Reboot and select IceWM from the LightDM WM menu. From the IceWM Menu → Settings → Themes → NanoBlue.

Use **PCManFM** to find **Configuration Files** in the ~**/.icewm** directory and edit them with **Mousepad**:

General	~/.icewm/preferences
Theme	~/.icewm/themes/<name>/default.theme
Menu	~/.icewm/menu
Shortcut Keys	~/.icewm/keys
App Launcher	~/.icewm/toolbar

Menu → Utility → FileTools → **File Manager PCManFM**
Ctrl + H, is the Hidden File toggle. Right click on a configuration file and select **Mousepad**. Use Find, Ctrl + F, to search for features. Be sure to Ctrl + S to save changes.

Pin an App to the Taskbar

From /usr/share/icons/gnome-brave/scalable copy the following icons to ~**/.icewm/icons**,:
 /places/folder.svg
 /devices/video-display.svg
 /categories/preferences-system-networking.svg
 Rename preferences-system-networking.svg to network.svg.

Menu → Utility → FileTools → **File Manager PCManFM**
Right click ~/.icewm/**toolbar** and select **Mousepad**.
Each entry will have four values:
 prog <ToolTip-Name> <Icon-Name> <Program-Name>

Comment out all the lines by placing a # at the beginning of the line, except for the line for "**x-www-browser**". Then add the the following three lines to the bottom of the file:
```
prog PCManFM folder.svg pcmanfm
prog XTerm video-display.svg xterm
prog Connman network.svg connman-gtk
```

Restart IceWM, from a terminal: To exit IceWM:
```
icewm -r
```
                                   Menu → Logout

TWM

TWM running Connman and Synaptic.

TWM in combination with Dmenu and Nitrogen produces a minimalist Desktop. The example ~/.twm**rc** file is a Run Command file used to configure TWM. Right clicking the Desktop launches **Dmenu**. Left clicking launches a menu to restore the **Wallpaper** or **Exit**. Run Nitrogen to select a Wallpaper.

For Windows that have a Title Bar, the left most icon is the **minimize** button, to **restore** reselect it from the **Icon Manager List**. The right most icon **resizes**, click and hold the icon to resize. A window must be pulled up and to the right before it can be pushed inward.

It will be necessary to launch some apps from a terminal:
```
sudo synaptic
connman-gtk --no-icon
gnome-screenshot -i
man twm
```
Closing the terminal
will close the app.
TWM documentation.

Install: twm, suckless-tools, nitrogen
Then create **twmrc** below and the **M** script (Page 214).

~/.twmrc

```
# Use Icon Manager as a Window List.
ShowIconManager
IconifyByUnmapping
# Desktop Right Click launches Dmenu.
Button1 = : root : f.menu "Exit"
Button3 = : root : ! "M &"

menu "Exit"
{
    "Menu" f.title
    "Wallpaper" f.exec "nitrogen --restore"
    "Logout" f.exec "killall twm"
}
Color
{
    DefaultForeground        "#FF0000"
    DefaultBackground        "#3333AA"
    BorderColor              "#000000"
    TitleForeground          "#DDDDDD"
    TitleBackground          "#3333AA"
    MenuForeground           "#DCDCDC"
    MenuBackground           "#494949"
    MenuBorderColor          "#494949"
    MenuShadowColor          "#FFFFFF"
    IconForeground           "#DDDDDD"
    IconBackground           "#3333AA"
    IconBorderColor          "#FF0000"
    IconManagerForeground    "#CCCCCC"
    IconManagerBackground    "#111155"
    IconManagerHighlight     "#FF0000"
}
```

Not a Desktop

XTerm / Tmux Split Screen

Install: xterm, tmux, suckless-tools

Create the **T**, **T2**, and **M** scripts:
/usr/bin/T
```
xrdb -merge ~/.Xresources; xterm -maximized &
```
/usr/bin/T2
```
lxterminal –gemoetry=300x100 &
```
/usr/bin/M
```
dmenu_run -fn 'Mono—18' &> /dev/null
```

From a terminal:
```
T
tmux
htop
```
Ctrl + B   Release then press %
```
neofetch
```
Ctrl + B   Release then press "   (Double Quote)
Ctrl + B   Release then press cursor Up
Ctrl + B + cursor Down   Release, repeat as needed.
Ctrl + B   Release then press cursor Down
```
cmatrix
```

214

tmux: - Terminal Multiplexer - To view a list of Short-cuts, press Ctrl + B, release then press ?, scroll or page up and down the list, Q to exit shortcuts. Shortcuts examples:
C-b t - means press Ctrl + B, release then press T.
C-b M-o - means press Ctrl + B, hold and press O.
C-b & - Ctrl + B, release, & exits Tmux, or **exit** command.
man tmux, tmux --help, YouTubes, Webpages

dmenu: - Side scrolling **suckless-tools** menu. Exits once a selection is made, pressing Esc also exits the menu.
man dmenu, dmenu --help, YouTubes, Webpages

ranger: - Ranger is a Console File Manger, use the cursor keys to navigate, press Enter to select. Selecting an image in Ranger launches the sxiv viewer. ? for help.
man ranger, ranger -- help, YouTubes, Webpages

sxiv: - Image Viewer - Add to bottom of: ~/.Xresources
   Sxiv.background: black   (See Page 50)
   Sxiv.foreground: white

gdu: - Pretty Fast Disk Usage Analyzer is a Console Disk Space Analyzer. gdu <directory>, gdu /, gdu ~, gdu -d. Scroll or page up and down, Enter to select, Q to Quit.
man gdu, gdu --help, YouTubes, Webpages

nitrogen: - Utility for changing and browsing wallpaper.
nitrogen --restore - Restores previous wallpaper.
man nitrogen, nitrogen --help, YouTubes, Webpages

tty-clock: Large Clock display with many options.
man tty-clock, tty-clock -h

caca-utils: ASCII Art, Esc to exit.
cacademo - ASCII demo, man cacademo
cacafire - ASCII Fire, man cacafire
cacaview <image> - ASCII Viewer, man cacaview

Console

Debian has seven preset virtual terminal Consoles. These can be invaluable in the event of a LightDM or Window Manager (WM) issue. Virtual Terminals (VTs) 2, 3, and 6 can be accessed by pressing Ctrl + Alt + Fn where n matches the VT, Ctrl + Alt + F6 for VT 6. VT7 is reserved for a GUI session which is where LightDM and the WMs run. Only one WM can run per user, however one user can have more than one GUI session. startx can also be used to start a WM for example: startx startlxde

VTs example:

Ctrl + Alt + F6	Jump to VT 6.
Alt + F5	Jump to VT 5.
Enter	Tap Enter, wake up VT.
Sign in.	Enter id and password.
startx xterm	Start X session.
T	Run T script Page 214.
M	Run Dmenu script.
galcu Enter	Launch Galculator.
W	Shows who is logged on.
Alt + →	Jump right, to VT6.
Alt + F7	Return to VT7.
sudo chvt 5	From a terminal.
File → Quit	Use the mouse.
Exit	Close XTerm.
Exit	Log out of VT5.
Alt + F7	Return to VT7.

The default number of VTs is 6. VT7 is the GUI default. To change the number of VTs, edit /etc/systemd/logind.conf and set **NAutoVTs** to the desired number of VT's.

AUTOMATION & VM

For this section of the book **use a test chip**. Do **NOT** perform the exercises in this section using your primary chip or primary storage.

Given the complexity of an operating system, it follows that it's initialization, init process, would also be complex. The evolution of the init process into a full automation system such as **systemd** is a natural progression.

While the over design and under documentation of systemd feels nefarious, it does offer some brilliant ideas. Its comforting to know its tempered by a distro's ability to fork or all together dump a project such as systemd.

systemd's corporate parent sees systemd as an umbrella term for a never ending line of software. Thusly systemd has many disemboweled components with uses ranging from setting the system clock to managing system logs. There are additional packages such as the Cockpit web interface and Anisble server automation. The cumulative effect of this is highly dispersed documentation.

systemctl

The work done by **systemd** is broken up into **units**. **systemctl -t help** will display a complete list of unit types. **list-units --type=<unit-type>** will display a list of that unit type. systemd will try to achieve the state defined by the default target, which can be found with **get-default**. **cgroups** short for control groups are used to regulate uses of system resources. A **service** aka daemon is a program run by the system as opposed to the user to carry out a task. A **scope** is a group of related programs. A **slice** is a hierarchy of scopes and services. When a list is returned, use the cursor Up / Down keys to roll thru the list and Q to quit.

From a terminal:

```
sudo su
systemctl --state=failed
systemctl reset-failed
systemctl --state=failed
systemctl -t help
systemctl list-units --type=socket
systemctl -t help
systemctl list-units --type=target
systemctl get-default
systemctl list-dependencies graphical.target
systemd-cgls
systemd-cgtop
systemctl -t help
systemctl list-units --type=service
systemctl list-units --type=service | grep dm
systemctl status lightdm.service
systemctl cat lightdm.service
systemclt stop lightdm.service        (Black Screen)
Alt + Ctrl + Del                      (Reboot)
```

Apache HTTP Server

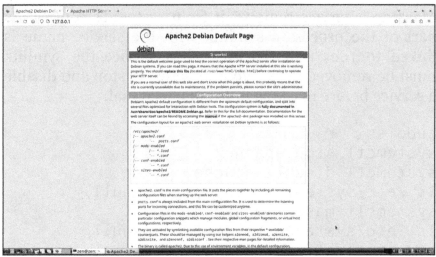

Apache HTTP Server 127.0.0.1

Apache HTTP Server example, from a terminal:

```
sudo su
apt list apache2
apt install apache2
apt install apache2-doc
```
Open a browser and go to the URL: localhost or 127.0.0.1
Go offline and open a second tab with the URL:
file:///usr/share/doc/apache2-doc/manual/en/index.html
```
systemctl show apache2          (From the terminal.)
systemctl cat apache2
systemctl edit apache2
```
Under the line: Anything between here and . . . . . . Add:
```
  [Service]
  ExecStartPre=mkdir -p /var/log/apache2
systemctl daemon-reload
systemctl show apache2
```

mkdir compensates for no previous logs, see Page 239.

Masking

Masking a service removes it from systemd's control. As part of the process a symlink with the service name is linked to /dev/null. To unmask a service the symlink must be removed. It is a good practice to stop and disable a service before masking it. From a terminal:

```
sudo su
systemctl stop apache2
systemctl disable apache2
ls /etc/systemd/system | grep null
systemclt mask apache2
ls /etc/systemd/system | grep null
systemctl status apace2

rm /etc/systemd/system/apache2.service
systemctl daemon-reload
systemctl enable apache2
systemctl start apache2
systemctl status apache2
```

Documentation

From a terminal:

```
ls /usr/bin/systemd*
ls /usr/bin/*ctl
ls /usr/sbin/*ctl
apt list cockpit
apt list ansible
```

Websites:

systemd.io
github.com/systemd
opointer.net/blog   (zero)
cockpit-project.org
ansible.com

redhat.com/sysadmin/intro-cockpit

Google: systemd access.redhat / developers.redhat

Virtualization

The computer power of yesterday that filled an entire room now fits in your phone. Along with the trends of smaller, cheaper, and increased power are digitization and convergence. The phone is a camera and the TV is a computer monitor. A mini PC is little larger than a phone and a growing number of phones have a computer desktop mode. Book, music, and movie collections are becoming virtualized.

Computer technology itself is becoming virtualized as computers become more standardized and modularized. Beowulfs were created to organize a cluster of computers. Now a single computer may be used to run a large number of containerized applications, such as Kubernetes.

Terms

UEFI is the successor to **BIOS**, the **firmware** between the software and the hardware. **KVM** provides support for virtualization and works with **QEMU** which is often wrapped by a GUI like **VMM** or **AQEMU**. **OVMF** implements **TinaoCore** in **QEMU**.

BIOS – Basic Input Output System
UEFI – Unified Extensible Firmware Interface
KVM – Linux Kernel based Virtual Machine
QEMU – Quick Emulator
OVMF – Open Virtual Machine Firmware
TinaoCore – Open Source UEFI
TCG – Tiny Code Generator - When KVM is not available.
VMM – Virtual Machine Manager

AQEMU – A frontend for QEMU

AQEMU is a GUI front-end to QEMU. In this section Debian will be installed on a virtual system using the already downloaded Debian Live ISO file. Installing AQEMU will install all the necessary software, the **Debian Live ISO** should be copied to the **Downloads** folder.

Install: aqemu

To **reset AQEMU**, delete the following two folders. This will not harm AQEMU, but it will be necessary to repeat the basic setup:

~/.aqemu   ~/.config/aqemu

The first time AQEMU is run, or has been reset, a **First Start Wizard** will run. Menu → System Tools → AQEMU

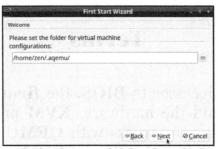

Accept the default VM folder by clicking **Next**.

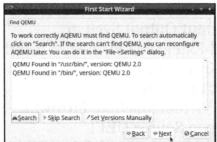

For **Find QEMU**, click **Search**, wait for it, then **Next**.

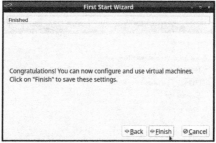

Click the **Finish** button to complete the setup.

Click **Add new VM** (green plus sign icon) top left.
This will launch a **New Virtual Machine Wizard**.

Click **Next** to accept the **Typical** default.

Click **Next** to accept the **Linux 2.6** default.

Click **Next** to accept the **KVM** default.

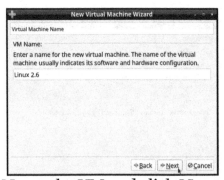

Name the VM and click **Next**.

Select a disk size, 10GB minimum, and click **Next**.

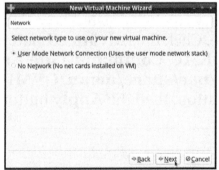

Click **Next** to accept the **Network** default.

Click **Finish** to complete the setup.

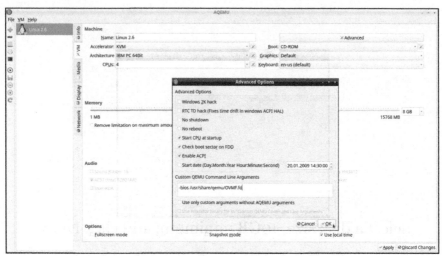

Select the **VM** tab to customize the VM.

CPU and memory can be adjusted here. UEFI firmware is configured here. Click the **Advanced** button, top right, in the **Custom QEMU Command Line Arguments** box enter: **-bios /usr/share/qemu/OVMF.fd**
Click the **OK** button, then the **Apply** button.

From the **Media** tab under **Add Devices**, click the **Add CD/DVD-ROM** button. In the **Properties** box click the **Browse** button and select the Debian Live ISO from the **Downloads** folder. Click the **OK** and **Apply** buttons.

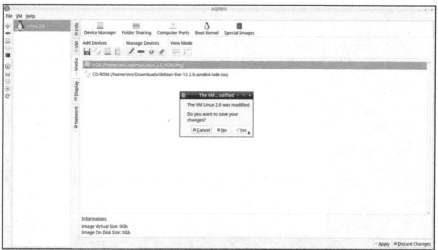

Click the **Start** button (Play icon), left side of the screen.

Click the **Yes** button to save changes. A virtual display will open and the VM will boot from the virtual CD/DVD-ROM.
Alt + Ctrl + G – Grab Input toggle.
Alt + Ctrl + F – Fullscreen toggle.
Avoid using Fullscreen during the install and boot processes, as the size will fluctuate which can crash QEMU.

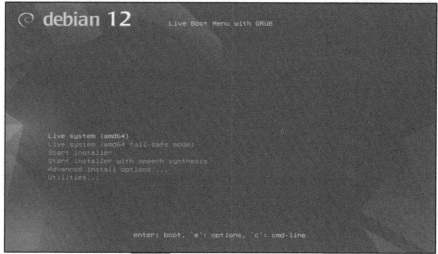

Press Enter to boot the **Live system**.

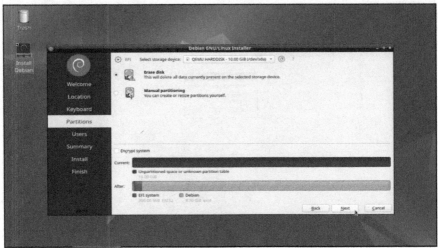

Click the Desktop **Install Debian** icon.

On the **Partitions** panel select **Erase Disk** and click the **Next** button. -OR- **Manual partitioning** see Page 21.

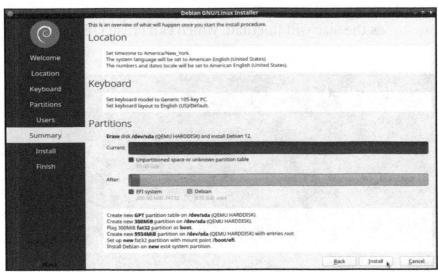

Summary panel, click the **Next** button.

The installation process can be monitored from the **Install** panel.

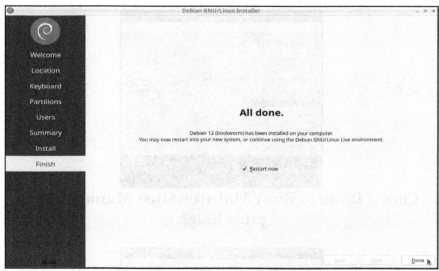

On the **Finish** panel click the **Done** button to reboot.

While the VM is booting tap the Esc key to open the **OVMF** menu. Note for later, once the VM is up: To shut-down the VM, from inside the VM shutdown Linux as normal. **Menu → Logout**. Notice the VM's time clock will be off, which will cause software install issues. With the **VM down**, on the **VM** tab uncheck Use local time.

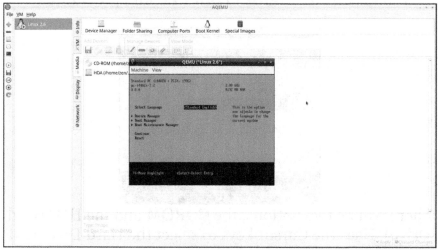

The **OVMF** menu.

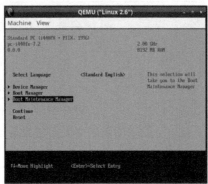

Cursor Down to **Boot Maintenance Manager** and press Enter.

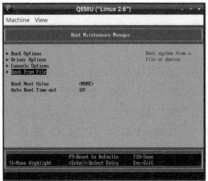

Cursor Down to **Boot From File** and press Enter.

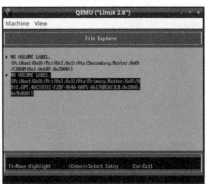

There will be two options, the CDROM and the HD (Hard Drive). Uses the Cursor keys to select the Hard Drive and press Enter.

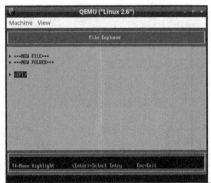

Cursor Down to **EFI** and press Enter.

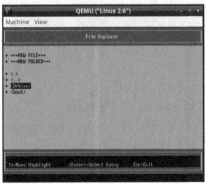

Cursor Down to **Debian** and press Enter.

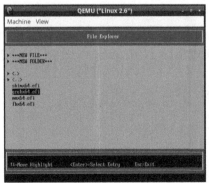

Cursor Down to **grubx64.efi** and press Enter.

Debian Boots!

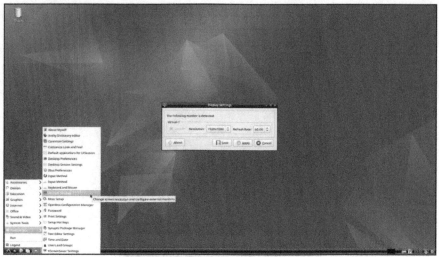

Menu → Preferences → **Monitor Settings**

Set the VM **Monitor Settings** to the same value as the actual System **Monitor Settings**. Toggle Fullscreen, (press `Alt` + `Ctrl` + `F`). It may be necessary to toggle Fullscreen twice for it to take affect.

/etc/resolv.conf

If the VM doesn't have internet, point **/etc/resolv.conf** to the Google Domain Name Servers (DNS).

From a terminal:
```
sudo su
cd /etc
mv resolv.conf resolv.bak
nano resolv.conf
  nameserver 8.8.8.8
  nameserver 8.8.4.4
```
`Ctrl` + `O`, Enter, `Ctrl` + `X`

OVMF

The save function of OVMF is currently broken upstream, meaning it will be necessary to continue to tap `Esc` while booting and navigate to the Debian grubx64.efi file in order to boot the VM. Once the save function has been fixed, it will be possible to add a boot option for the grubx64.efi file and give it priority in the boot order:

Boot Maintenance Manager
Boot Options
Add Boot Option
Navigate to the grubx64.efi file.
Name the boot option.
Commit Changes and Exit
Change Boot Order
Commit Changes and Exit

This is provided as reference and does NOT currently work.

Documentation

AQEMU is a collaboration of several projects. AQEMU's built-in help, **Help → Menu** or **F1** contains links to documentation. The QEMU command constructed by AQEMU can be displayed by clicking the **Show QEMU Arguments** button just above the **Start** button. This can be copied into a text file and run as a script.

The From a terminal:
```
man kvm
which qemu-system-x86_86
ls /usr/bin/qemu*
man qemu-system-x86_64
qemu-system-x86_64 --help
```

Websites:
linux-kvm.org
qemu.org
uefi.org
tianocore.org

VMM

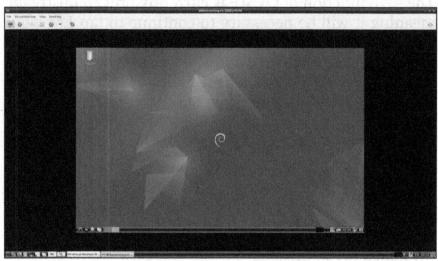

VMM runing Debian 12

Virtual Machine Manager VMM is the GUI front-end for libvirt. VMM's corporate parent has set an EOL (End Of Life) for VMM within it's own distro. It's network configuration is more suited to more experienced users. With VMM it is <u>not</u> necessary to catch OVMF during the boot process by pressing Esc and navigate the OVMF menu to start the VM.

Install: virt-manager

From a terminal:
```
cat /etc/group | grep virt
getent group
sudo usermod -aG libvirt <user-id>
```

Documentation: virt-manager.org -- help
man virt-manager, virt-manager.org

New VM installs by default will select **BIOS** for Firmware. The **Firmware** must manually be set to **UEFI**. At the end of the **Create a new virtual machine** setup, check the **Customize configuration before install** box.

Check **Customize configuration**

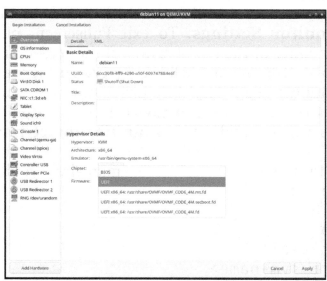

For Firmware select **UEFI**.

From the VMM home screen **Edit** menu, select **Connection Details**. In the **Connection Details** panel, check the **Autostart On Boot** check box. This will insure the virtual network starts before the VM.

Check Autostart On Boot

For Fullscreen, View → **Fullscreen**. The VM's **Monitor Settings** can be set to the same value as the actual System **Monitor Settings**. To exit Fullscreen, place the mouse pointer at the top of center of the screen, from the drop down icon menu, click the **Leave fullscreen** icon. To shutdown the VM, from inside the VM shutdown Linux as normal. **Menu → Logout**. Disk image files for the VMs can be found here: **/var/lib/libvirt/images**

From a terminal: man virsh, virsh --help
```
sudo su
virsh
help
list --all
start <vm-name>
exit
virt-viewer
```
Click the **Connect** button.

Cockpit

From a browser: localhost:9090

Cockpit is an all-in-one system for managing the performance, automation, and software for remote physical and virtual systems. It may be considered an extension of the systemd software family.

It is infamous for attempting to push the methodologies of it's corporate parent into other distros. It is currently known to cause network issues.

Cockpit uses a web interface and is accessed using a browser, the default URL is localhost:9090. Sign in with your Linux id and password.

Install: cockpit, cockpit-machines, cockpit-podman
         cockpit-doc, realmd, spice-vdagent

Documentation: cockpit-project.org, man cockpit
         /usr/share/doc/cockpit/guide/guide.html

The **Overview** home screen.

To enable full functionality, click the **Turn on administrative access** button. It will be necessary to renter the user password again.

Cockpit will automatically load any VMs created by VMM into the **Virtual machines** panel. Clicking the **Launch remote viewer** button will download a link that opens the remote viewer when clicked. Once the download link has been clicked it will be deleted.

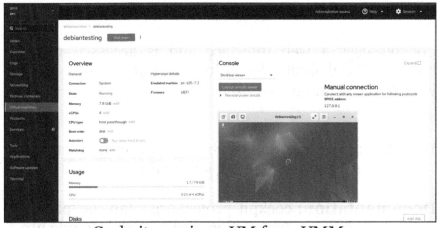

Cockpit running a VM from VMM.

Viewing Logs

dmesg displays the kernel log messages. The systemd journal can be viewed with the **journalctl** command. The **--list-boots** option will list boot logs. Use the **-b** option to view a log file, zero for the current log and negative numbers for previous boots. The **-x** option offers explanations and possible solutions to messages. Use the Cursor Up / Down keys to scroll and Q to quit. Use the **-f** option, to view live log messages. **systemd-cat** sends output to the systemd journal. From LXTerminal:

```
sudo su
  dmesg
  journalctl --list-boots
  Q
  journalctl -b 0
  Q
  journalctl -b 0 -x
  Q
  journalctl --help
  Q
  journalctl -f
  Ctrl + C
  systemd-cat ls -l
  journalctl -b 0 | tail -20
exit
```

Changes made to the /etc/fstab file will prevent logs from being saved between reboots. To save logs comment out or delete the 3 tmpfs lines added on Page 25.

Check a program's man page, programs may keep their own log files. It maybe helpful to start a program from the command line. Copy a program's start command from the LXDE menu. **Menu** → right click on the **App** → **Properties** → **Desktop Entry tab**, copy Ctrl + C the **Command** and paste it Ctrl + Shift + V into LXTerminal. Any errors will likely show up in LXTerminal.

AppArmor

AppArmor is a kernel security module that can be used to limit a programs access to resources. AppArmor is installed and enabled by default. The **aa-apparmor-utils** tools used to control it must be manually installed.

Install: aa-apparmor-utils

AppArmor can not provide an individual status. Improperly configured AppArmor profiles can result in permission denied errors. Complain / Enforce can be used to test for AppArmor issues. Log files can provide helpful details. **Complain** can be used to disable AppArmor for a specific program, the full path to the program is required. **Enforce** is used to enable AppArmor for a specific program, the full path to the program is required. Most profiles can be found in /etc/apparmor.d. From a terminal:

```
sudo su
  man apparmor
  man aa-status
  aa-status --help
  aa-complain --help
  aa-enforce --help
  ls /etc/apparmor.d
  which man
  aa-status
  aa-complain /usr/bin/man
  aa-status
  aa-enforce /usr/bin/man
  aa-status
exit
```

Q to Quit man.

Look for **man** "/usr/bin/man" in the aa-status list.

BACKUPS

The **Debian Live** chip is a great way to test Debian before installing it. The Debian Live chip can also be used to create a **Full Backup & Recovery System** or a **Portable Linux System** on a chip. These chips are not tuned to any specific system and should boot on any Intel/AMD based PC or Laptop. Disable Secure Boot, if enabled, when using a Live USB Stick, this process varies with manufacture and model.

These systems will not have the performance of standard systems, but will be portable. For Backup chips 256 GB is a good minimum size, the larger the chip the more backups it will hold. For Portable chips, 128 GB is a good minimum size.

The Debian Live **persistence** option is what allows a Debian Live system to retain it's data. This allows backup utilities and settings such as WiFi configurations to be retained. These chips can be used to install, repair, backup, and restore a Linux system. They can even be used as a portable Linux System. An entire Linux toolbox that fits on a key-chain for the price of a USB stick.

Debian Live Persistence

There are some particularities to creating a Debian Live System. As a standard, when PCs and Laptops are booting they can read FAT32 and ISO images by default. They can not read Linux formats such as ext4 until after they have booted. Debian is distributed as an ISO file, which contains symlinks. FAT32 does not support symlinks. Because a USB stick can not boot as an ISO and have additional partitions, it must boot from FAT32. Xarchiver should be able to translate the symlinks and copy the Debian ISO files into a FAT32 partition. If Xarchiver fails, use 7z (Page 12).

Partition	Type & Size	Contents
BOOT Boot flag on.	FAT32 4GB	Debian Live
persistence persistence.conf / union	ext4 4GB / Backup 20GB / Portable	Debian Live Data
data	ext4 Remaining Space	Backups Data Files

4 Requirements to Enable Persistence
- Start Linux with the persistence option.
- A partition named persistence.
- A file name persistence.conf in it's root directory.
- The conf file must contain / union (/ space union).

Building a Backup System Overview

Create a **hold** directory: ~/**hold**
Using **GParted** format a USB stick:
   Insert the USB stick, find the stick in GParted.
   If mounted, unmount the partitions.
   Delete any existing partitions.
   Create a GUID Partition Table (GPT)

Create 3	BOOT	FAT32	4GB
partitions:	persistence	ext4	4GB
	data	ext4	Remaining Space

Remove and reinsert the USB stick.
From a terminal: **sudo pcmanfm**
   Grant access to **persistence** and **data**.
   Disable ext4 journaling for **persistence** and **data**.
   df -h
   debugfs -R features /dev/sdxx
   tune2fs -O ^has_journal /dev/sdxx
Using **Xarchiver** extract ISO files to **hold** directory.
   Select: **With full path**
   Uncheck: **Ensure a containing directory**
Using **PCManFM** copy the **splash png** files;
   From: ~/hold/isolinux
   To: ~/hold/boot/grub
Use **Mousepad** to edit ~/hold/boot/grub/grub.cfg
   Edit first line to start with "**linux**" (line 5).
   Add **persistence** and delete **quiet** and **splash**.
   From: ... boot= live components **quiet splash** ...
   To: ... boot=live **persistence** components ...
Copy files From: ~/**hold** To: **BOOT** partition.
In the **persistence** partition:
   Create **persistence.conf** file in root.
    / union
Using **GParted** set the boot partition boot flag.

Building a Backup System

First create a directory named **hold** in the home directory
~/**hold**

Install: gparted

Menu → System Tools → GParted

Click the top right pull-down to view
the available drives.

Insert the USB stick. From the **GParted**
menu, top left, select **Refresh Devices**.

Click the top right pull-down to view
the available drives. In this example
/dev/sdb is the inserted USB stick.

Delete any partitions on the USB stick, right click on the partition and selecting **Delete**. If **Delete** is grayed out then the **Unmount** option will likely not be grayed out and there will be a **key** icon between the **Partiton** and the **Name** indicating the the partition is mounted.

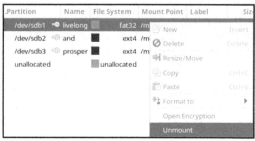

Unmount any mounted partitions.

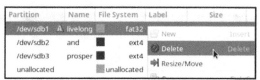

Delete any partitions on the USB stick.

Click the **Apply All Operations** green check mark at the top of the screen. Click **Apply** in the pop-up.

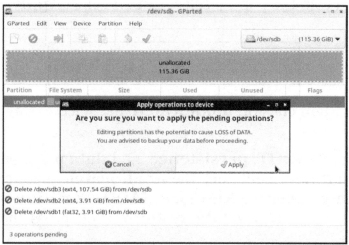

Click the **Apply** button in the pop-up.

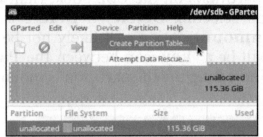

Device → **Create Partition Table**

From the pop-up select **gpt** and click **Apply**.

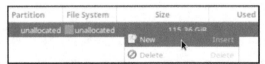

Right click on **unallocated** and select **New**.

Create the **BOOT**, **persistence**, and **data** partitions. For each partition, right click the **unallocated** space and select **New**. Enter the **New size (MIB)**, **Partition name**, **Label**, and select a **File system**. Then press the **Add** button.

No changes will be made until the **Apply All Operations** green check mark at the top of the screen has been clicked. It's ok to delete and re-enter a partition.

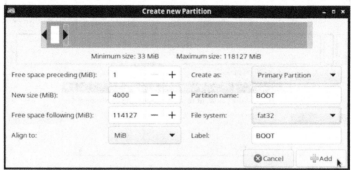

BOOT, 4000 MIB, fat32

persistence, 4000 MIB, ext4

data, remaining space, ext4

Click the **Apply All Operations** green check mark at the top of the screen. Click **Apply** in the pop-up.

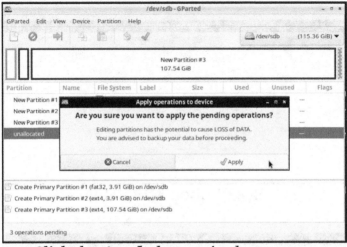

Click the **Apply** button in the pop-up.

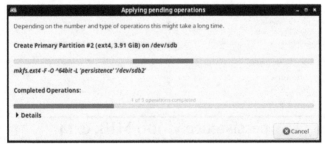

The process will take time, allow it to finish.

When the process is complete, click the **Close** button.

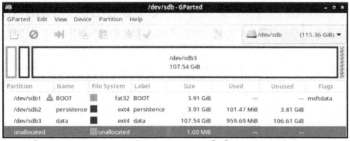

The BOOT, persistence, and data partitions.

Close **GParted** and remove the **USB** stick. Wait for a moment then reinsert the **USB** stick. There will be a pop-up for each partition. For each pop-up click the **OK** button, this will open a **PCManFM** window for each partition. Close all **PCManFM** windows.

From a terminal: `sudo pcmanfm` From **PCManFM** navigate to the **/media/<user-id>** folder. Right click on **data**, select **Properties**, **Permissions** tab, from the **Change content** pull-down select **Anyone,** then click the **OK** button, click **Yes** for the pop-up. Repeat the process for the **persistence** folder.

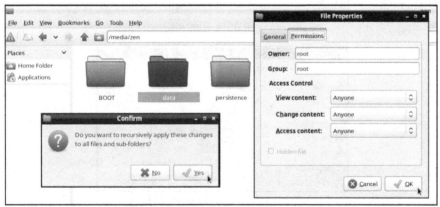

From the **Change content** pull-down select **Anyone**.

Close **PCManFM** and continue from the terminal. Turn OFF **ext4 journaling** for the **persistence** and **data** partitions. **debugfs** displays the partition features, **tune2fs** -O (Capital letter O not a zero.) is used to turn a feature on or off. The "^", caret means OFF, **no** "^", caret means ON. **df -h** displays the mounted partitions. Continuing with **/dev/sdb** as an example. From a terminal:

```
sudo su
df -h
umount /dev/sdb2
umount /dev/sdb3
debugfs -R features /dev/sdb2
tune2fs -O ^has_journal /dev/sdb2
debugfs -R features /dev/sdb2
debugfs -R features /dev/sdb3
tune2fs -O ^has_journal /dev/sdb3
debugfs -R features /dev/sdb3
```

Close the **terminal** and open **PCManFM**, navigate to the **Debian ISO**, for this example the ISO is in the **Downloads** folder. Right click on the **Debian ISO** and select **Xarchiver**.

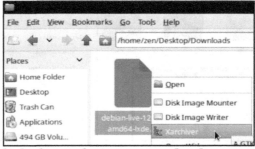

Right click the Debain ISO and select Xarchiver.

The Debian ISO will open in Xarchiver. Extract the files and place them in the ~/hold folder.

Action → Extract

In the **Extract files** pop-up:
For **Extract to**
   Select the **hold** folder
For **Files**
   Select **All files**
For **File Paths**
   Select **With full path**

Click the **Extract** button. This will take a few minutes. The processing indicator at the bottom right will flash red / green while it is extracting and solid green when done.

Close Xarchiver. Copy the splash png files from isolinux to boot/grub and edit grub.cfg From a terminal:

```
cp ~/hold/isolinux/splash* ~/hold/boot/grub
mousepad ~/hold/boot/grub/grub.cfg
```

Edit the first line to start with the word linux, remove **quiet** and **splash** and add **persistence** before components.

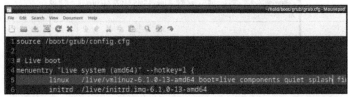

```
... boot=live components quiet splash ...
```

```
... boot=live persistence components ...
```

Save the file and close Mousepad. Continuing from the terminal. Copy the files from **hold** to **BOOT**, this will take some time. The **copy -r** option means recursively, include all the sub directories. From a terminal:

```
cp -r ~/hold/* /media/<user-id>/BOOT
```

Create the **persistence.conf** file in the **persistence** partition. It must contain **/ union**, slash space union, and press Enter. Not pressing Enter would be like typing a command at a terminal and never pressing Enter, nothing would happen. Create the **persistence.conf** file. From a terminal:

```
mousepad /media/<user-id>/persistence/persistence.conf
```
/ union

Save the file and close Mousepad.

Use **GParted** to set the **BOOT** partition's **boot** flag. Right click on the **BOOT** partition and select **Manage Flags**. From the list of flags check **boot**, this will automatically check **esp** and uncheck **msftdata**. Then click the **Close** button to update the **BOOT** flags. When a boot flag is set, a partition can not be mounted or edited. If it becomes necessary to edit the **BOOT** partition, unchecking the **boot** flag will reverse the flag settings. Some systems can boot without the **boot** flag, but it is a good practice to set it.

Click on **boot** to check mark it.
Then click the **Close** button to update.

Two Modes of Operation

The USB **Backup stick** can be booted **with persistence** and used as a **backup** or **portable system**. Or, it can be booted **without persistence** and used to **install Debian**.

The **Backup stick** has been configured to boot with persistence. To boot without persistence, press **E** to edit the GRUB boot option. Cursor **Right** to place the cursor under the **p** in **persistence**, tap **Delete** to remove the word **persistence**. Then **Ctrl** + **X** or **F10** to boot.

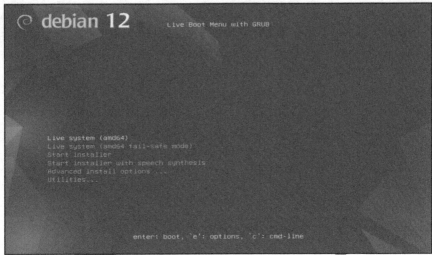

Press Enter to boot with **persistence** or E to Edit.

Pressing E to Edit

GNU GRUB version 2.06-13

```
setparms 'Live system (amd64)

      linux           /live/vmlinuz-6.1.0-13-amd64 boot=live persistence com\
ponents findisos=${iso_path}
      initrd          /live/initrd.img-6.1.0-13-amd64
```

Minimum Emacs-like screen editing is supported. TAB lists
completions. Press Ctrl+x of F10 to boot. Ctrl-c or F2 for a
command-line or ESC to discard edits and return to the GRUB men.

Enter: boot, 'e': options, 'c': cmd-line

Press E to Edit the GRUB boot command. Use this mode when installing Debian. Lines ending in a **backslash **, are continued on the next line. Cursor Right to reach the **p** in **persistence**. Then tap Delete to remove the word **persistence**. Press Ctrl + X or F10 to boot. Run the Debian Installer.

Booting with Persistence

Booting with persistence allows backup software to be installed and retained. Any cheat sheets, notes, or Tiddly Wikis should be copied to the **data** partition. Any configurations change will also be retained.

Install: fsarchiver, gparted, htop, neofetch, screenfetch
When using **Live USB sticks**: Kernel updates wont work. Most unusual error / warning messages can be ignored when installing software.

3 Backup sticks are a good minimum of Backup sticks. It is a good practice to rotate Backup sticks so all current backups are not on the same Backup stick. Stylizing desktops with wallpapers and colors can be a useful reminder of which Backup stick is in use. Label guns are a practical way to label USB sticks. It can be time saving to keep a mini notebook with a list of backups showing what was backed up, when, and which USB stick was used.

A plain text file cheat sheet can be handy:

```
df -h
umount /dev/sdb2
debugfs -R features /dev/sdb2
tune2fs -O ^has_journal /dev/sdb2

/etc/fstab
tmpfs  /var/log  tmpfs  defaults,noatime  0  0
tmpfs  /var/tmp  tmpfs  defaults,noatime  0  0
tmpfs  /tmp      tmpfs  defaults,noatime  0  0

fsarchiver savefs /media/user/data/arc.fsa /dev/sdb1
fsarchiver restfs /media/user/data/arc.fsa id=0,/dev/sdb1
fsarchive archinfo /media/user/data/arc.fsa
```

mytips.txt

Using the Backup Stick

Tips top left, PCManFM top right, Terminal bottom.

It's a good practice to organizing screens before starting. It's convenient to have a cheat sheet out along with a view of the backup being created and a terminal.

A FAT32 partition with the boot flag turned on should not mount. Backing up a Debian system on a micro SD card connected by a USB adapter with no swap partition (sdb – sdb1/ sdb2 in this example), would work like this:

Start the Backup system.
Insert the USB adapter with the micro SD card.
Organize screens.
From a terminal:
  sudo su
  df -h
  umount /dev/sdb2   (umount sdb1 if mounted.)
  fsarchiver savefs /media/user/data/book.fsa /dev/sdb1 /dev/sdb2

To restore:
  fsarchiver restfs /media/user/data/arc.fsa id=0,/dev/sdb1 id=1,/dev/sdb2

FSArchiver is used to backup (**savefs**) and restore (**restfs**) a file system. For information about a backup use **archinfo**. For more information about fsarchiver:
man fsarchiver, sudo fsarchiver --help

To view information about a backup:
sudo fsarchiver archinfo /media/user/data/book.fsa

```
===================== archive information ===============
Archive type:                    filesystems
Filesystems count:               2
Archive id:                      660653b5
Archive file format:             FsArCh_002
Archive created with:            0.8.7
Archive creation date:           2024-04-04_11-24-55
Archive label:                   <none>
Minimum fsarchiver version:      0.6.4.0
Compression level:               8 (zstd level 8)
Encryption algorithm:            none

==================== filesystem information ============
Filesystem id in archive:    0
Filesystem format:           vfat
Filesystem label:            BOOT
Filesystem uuid:             988A04A3
Original device:             /dev/sdb1
Original filesystem size: 3.90 GB (4186103808 bytes)
Space used in filesystem:        15.66 MB (16424960 bytes)

==================== filesystem information ============
Filesystem id in archive:    1
Filesystem format:           ext4
Filesystem label:            main
Filesystem uuid:             e39219d8-803d-4bd8-9cbb-881567c4cbff
Original device:             /dev/sdb2
Original filesystem size: 54.63 GB (58660610048 bytes)
Space used in filesystem:        20.12 GB (21601255424 bytes)
```

The **Filesystem id in archive** and **Original device** are used when restoring. Do not backup swap partitions. If the structure of partitions on a device is unclear, GParted can be used to examine the partitions.

Chip Considerations

Portable systems (non-Backup Systems) can have much larger persistence partitions, 20GB is a good minimum size. A data partition (can be any name) is not required, but it is a good practice to keep a copy of important files outside of the persistence partition.

Retiring an SD card after a year is a great way to make an annual backup. SD cards can last for years.

To select a few files from a restore, a backup can be restored to a temporary chip, and the select files can be copied from that chip.

Live systems will not have the performance of normal installed system. Using old USB sticks can be extremely slow.

If the write light of a USB stick is on the underside of the stick, a cosmetic travel mirror can be used.

Just the wrong combination of SD card, card reader, and software version may fail to read an SD card. Newer SD cards may also have issues with older card readers. In either case, the solution is to buy an updated card reader.

Two chips with the same UUID's (Universally Unique Identifier) can not be mounted on the same system at the same time. **sudo blkid** will display the UUID's in use on a system. By default FSArchiver will restore using the UUID's of the original chip when restoring. This can be overridden using the UUID option (uuid=<new-id>).

LOOSE ENDS

The free range nature of Linux allows it to evolve as need and often in several directions at one time. **"If you don't like it, fork it."** is pillar of open source software. A visit to distrowatch.com for and idea of how may distros there are.

Two major trends in Linux that touch virtually every system are the move from X.org to Wayland and the move from initd to Systemd:

- X.org to Wayland - Interface, displays, etc.
- initd to Systemd - Start up, shutdown, automation.

Debian Handbook Page 62
Debian Reference Card Page 278
Advanced BASH-Scripting Page 125

Also available from Synaptic, the Debian Reference, Installation Guide, and Maintenance Guide. Search on debian-reference, installation-guide, maint-guide. The ebooks can be found under /usr/share/doc/.

For forgotten passwords see Page 28.

Kali

Download the 64 bit Installer.

Kali Linux is popular with computer security specialists. There are several popular Linux distros such as Kali that are derived from Debian. The closer a derived distro is to Debian the more likely it's software will run on Debian and vice versa.

Kali Linux can be downloaded from the kali.org Installer webpage. Kali releases are identified by Year and Quarter, Kali Linux 2024.1 is January, 2024.4 is October. Kali and Debian USB sticks created from ISO files are created the same way (Page 8).

As always, test new software on a test chip before installing on a primary storage system. In the case of new Kali users, installing **Kali** in **AQEMU** may ease the process. If installing from an ISO USB stick fails, do try installing using AQEMU.

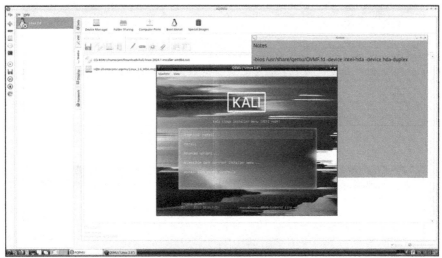

Kali **Graphical Install** in AQEMU.

If installing in AQEMU, (Page 222) in the text box for **Custom QEMU Command Line Arguments**, enter:
-bios /usr/share/qemu/OVMF.fd
-device intel-hda
-device hda-duplex

The **device** entries should enable sound. Wiggling the mouse every few minutes while installing will prevent the screen from going to sleep. The Kali **Graphical Install** will ask minimal questions and offer practical defaults.

Kali Partitions using the AQEMU Virtual Hard Drive.

Software selection defaults.

Continue

If installing Kali in **AQEMU**, don't deselect any software. Be sure to tap the `Esc` key while booting to bring up the **OVMF** menu:

> **OVMF** menu
> **Boot Maintenance Manager**
> **Boot From File**
> Select the **HD** not the the CDROM.
> **EFI**
> **kali**
> **grubx64.efi**

When using **AQEUM**, the **Grab Input** and **Fullscreen** shortcuts are important for navigation. Avoid using Fullscreen during the install and boot processes, as the size will fluctuate which can crash QEMU:

`Alt` + `Ctrl` + `G` – Grab Input toggle.
`Alt` + `Ctrl` + `F` – Fullscreen toggle.

Kali running in AQEMU

Menu → Settings → **Display**, can be used to adjust the display size. AQEMU users can set the display size to the actual display and then Alt + Ctrl + F – Fullscreen toggle.

From a terminal:
```
sudo apt update -y
sudo apt install synaptic -y
```

Menu → Usual Applications → System → **Synaptic Package Manager** Click the **Reload** button, top left. Install **alsa-utils**.

Preform a speaker test (Page 53), from a terminal:
```
speaker-test
```

Be sure to try **kali-undercover**. Run it a second time to return to normal.

Privacy Focused Linux

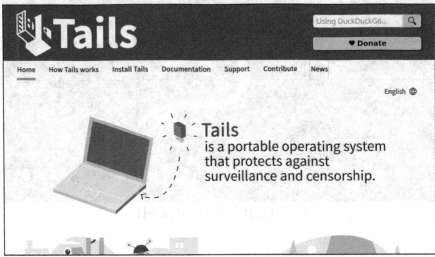

Tails OS

While Kali is focused on security testing, there are other security focused Linux distros that focus on privacy such as Tails. Finding a Linux distro that has been tailored to a specific task can have many benefits.

When using a public network it is a good practice to use a VPN, Virtual Private Network. VPN services are worth re-searching, among the many providers are DuckDuckGo, Google, Opera, Mozilla (Firefox), and Brave.

Security Focused YouTube Channels:
- youtube.com/@SecurityFWD
- youtube.com/@NullByteWHT
- youtube.com/@NaomiBrockwellTV

Managing Groups

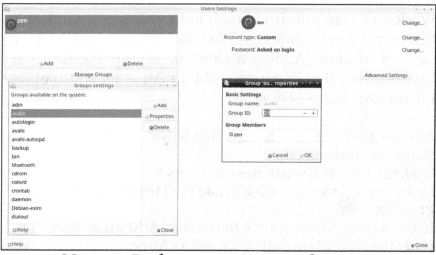

Menu → Preferences → Users and Groups

To display the user and groups a user belongs to, from a terminal:

```
id
groups
```

To change a users groups:
Menu → Preferences → **Users and Groups**
Click the **Manage Groups** button
In the Groups settings pop-up
   Select the desired Group
   Click the **Properties** button
In the Group Properties pop-up,
   Group Memembers section
   Check the checkbox to add the user.
   Uncheck the checkbox to remove the user.

More LXDE Shortcut Keys

While not common it is possible to position a window so the menu bar is inaccessible, making it a challenge to move a window. Adding a shortcut key for the move action resolves this situation. Add an Alt + F7 shortcut key for window move action:

Menu → Preferences → **Setup Hot Keys**
Select the **Actions** tab.
Click the toolbar **Create new actions** Icon.
In the pop-up window, click inside the **Hotkey 1** area.
Press Alt + F7.
In the pop-up window, click the toolbar **Add an action** icon.
From the Add action pull-down, select **Move**.
In the pop-up window, click the toolbar **Accept changes** icon
In the pop-up window, click the **Apply** button.
In the pop-up window, click the toolbar **Accept changes** icon
Click the toolbar **Save all changes . . .** button

More complex features which perform multiple actions at one time can be added by directly editing **lxde-rc.xml** file in the **~/.config/openbox** directory. Add a split window action, that uses the Win key and cursor keys. Open the **lxde-rc.xml** file in Mousepad and save it as **lxde-rc.bak**. Then reopen the **lxde-rc.xml** file, do a find Ctrl + F on F7. Just after:

```
<keybind key='A-F7'>
    <action name='Move'/>
</keybind>
```

Add the following lines, note the sections are repetitive, and can be copied and pasted to save time. When done, save an reboot. Win + Cursor key now splits the screen.

```
<keybind key='W-Right'>
    <action name='UnmaximizeFull'/>
    <action name='MoveResizeTO'>
        <width>50%</width>
    </action>
    <action name='MaximizeVert'/>
    <action name='MoveResizeTo'>
        <x>-0</x>
        <y>0</y>
    </action>
</keybind>
<keybind key='W-Left'>
    <action name='UnmaximizeFull'/>
    <action name='MoveResizeTO'>
        <width>50%</width>
    </action>
    <action name='MaximizeVert'/>
    <action name='MoveResizeTo'>
        <x>0</x>
        <y>0</y>
    </action>
</keybind>
<keybind key='W-Up'>
    <action name='UnmaximizeFull'/>
    <action name='MoveResizeTO'>
        <height>50%</height>
    </action>
    <action name='MaximizeHorz'/>
    <action name='MoveResizeTo'>
        <x>0</x>
        <y>0</y>
    </action>
</keybind>
<keybind key='W-Down'>
    <action name='UnmaximizeFull'/>
    <action name='MoveResizeTO'>
        <height>50%</height>
    </action>
    <action name='MaximizeHorz'/>
    <action name='MoveResizeTo'>
        <x>0</x>
        <y>-0</y>
    </action>
</keybind>
```

Alt + Ctrl + Del can be assigned to launch **lxde-logout**.

Developer Tools – Webpage Design

Firefox Developer Tools view of Notepad

From **Firefox** open the **Notepad** URL Page 181. Right click in the center of the display and select **Inspect (Q)**, this will open the **Developer Tools**. From the Developer Tools dot menu (top right) select **Separate Window**, then select **Show Split Console**. Using **PCManFM** right click on any image and select **Copy**, click in the center of the **Notepad** and **paste** (Ctrl + V). The Developer Tools screen will update. This is an embedded base64 text image. Double clicking the image text will select it so it can be copied Ctrl + C. Using Inspect(Q) text images can be copied from one webpage to another.

Use the following script to create a text image in mousepad, Ctrl + A, Ctrl + C to copy the text. **goTextPic** <image>
/usr/bin/goTextPic colon image, semicolon base64 comma

```
F=$1; E=${F#*.}
COMMAND='data:image/'$E';base64,'$(base64 -w0 $F)
echo $COMMAND > pic.txt; mousepad pic.txt &
```

Automa – Browser Automation

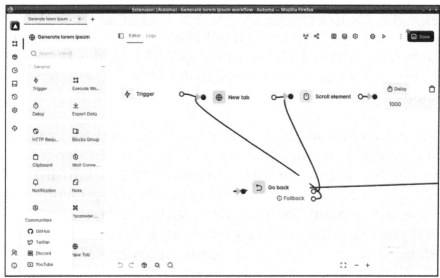

Firefox running Automa

Automa is an in browser automation that can be used to auto-fill forms, perform repetitive tasks, take screenshots and scrap data. The interface is exceptionally friendly and does not require programming.

Select **Add-ons** from the Firefox menu, then click on **Extensions**. Search for and install **Automa**. Grant any required permissions. Support can be found on the Automa website, as well as a growing number of YouTubes.

In Brower Automation

Automa	automa.site
Selenium Suite	selenium.dev
Greasemonkey	github.com/greasemonkey
Puppeteer	developer.chrome.com/docs/puppeteer
Tampermonkey	github.com/Tampermonkey

Unicode

Modern computers use Universal Character Sets (UCS) codes. UTF-8, Unicode Transformation Format 8-bit, is currently used by Debian. In Linux Ctrl + Shift + U is used to directly enter a characters using UTF-8 character hex codes.

Xpad is a convenient place to keep commonly used special characters. If a character can be copied it's hex code can be displayed using **printf <character> | hexdump**. To see what UCS is in used use the **locale -a** command. The **Character Map**, Menu → Accessories → Character Map, is a practical way to search for character codes. To search within a character set by name use **Search → Find**.

From a terminal:

Ctrl + Shift + U, 0040, Enter
Ctrl + Shift + U, 40, Enter
```
  echo -e '\u0040'
  printf @ | hexdump
  locale -a
  man utf8
  man ascii
  man charsets
  gucharmap            (Launches Character Map)
```

Character Map Commonly used Characters:
View By → Script → Common
View By → Unicode Block → All
View By → Unicode Block → Basic Latin

Go Scripts

Go scripts are a convention used in this book. Generally script names can be any name that does not conflict with a name already in use by the system. Go is easy to remember and few program names start with **go**. Wrapper scripts can be used to start programs, set variable, or issue commands before or after a program is run.

Scripts must be executable, **chmod +x** . If they are not in **$PATH**, the full path must be specified. "**./**" means the current working directory, **pwd**. /usr/bin is a good location for Go scripts. **which** shows the location of the script or program that will be run. **type** shows if there is more than program or script in $PATH. **file** shows the kind of file. **stat** shows file details.

From a terminal:
```
sudo su
  nano /usr/bin/godothis
    ls
    date
  Ctrl + O, Enter, Ctrl + X
  chmod +x godothis
  exit
cd ~
pwd
ls /usr/bin/go*
echo $PATH
which godothis
type godothis
file /usr/bin/godothis
stat /usr/bin/godothis
cat /usr/bin/godothis
```

Add MS Core Fonts

It's a good practice to backup the sources.list file before editing it. From a terminal:

```
cd /etc/apt                    If sources.bak exists
ls                             use bak2, bak3 etc.
sudo cp sources.list sources.bak
sudo nano sources.list
```

Add the repository sections **contrib** and **non-free** to the end of the line that ends with **bullseye main:**

deb https://deb.debian.org/debian bullseye main **contrib non-free**

–OR- Place them on their own line.

deb https://deb.debian.org/debian bullseye contrib

deb https://deb.debian.org/debian bullseye non-free

Save the file and exit nano. Then from a terminal:

```
sudo apt update -y
```

Start **Synaptic** and press the **Reload** button, top left. Search by name for **mscore**. Install ttf-mscorefonts-installer. Repositories can also be edited in Synaptic.

Synaptic Settings → **Repositories**

PC Linux to Android Linux

The PC PCManFM file manager can be used to move files directly into and out of UserLAnd's /storage/internal and /storages/sdcard folders. The PC can also be used to create the file path, if it doesn't exist.

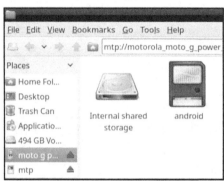

Select a drive and navigate to the **storage** folder.

PC	Android:
<device1>/Android/data/tech.ula/files/**storage**	/storage/internal
<device2>/Android/data/tech.ula/files/**storage**	/storage/sdcard

The pathway can be bookmarked in PCManFM, `Ctrl` + `D`, for convenience.

On the Android phone:
USB Preferences should be set to **File Transfer**.
USB Debugging should be turned **On**.
   This allows a PC greater access to the Android Device.

USB Debugging is available in the **Developer options**. To turn on **Developer options**, from settings:
   About phone
   Tap **Build number** repeatedly
   Developer options will activate.

ISO Master – ISO File Editor

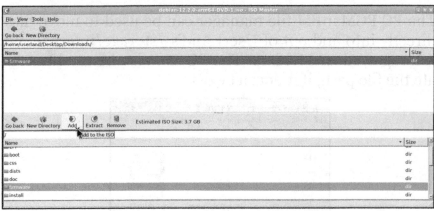

ISO Master editing an ISO file.

Install: isomaster

Description: ISO Master can be used to create and edit ISO image files. ISO Master will display ISO's on the bottom and file directories on the top. Highlight directory files and click **Add** to add them to the ISO. Highlight ISO files and click **Extract** to add them to the file directory. Be sure to save new ISO's when done: **File → Save As**

As of the writing of this book, Xarchiver is a more useful tool for working with ISO files than ISO Master. In the future that could change. ISO Master can not currently be used to create Live Debian chips with persistence, at this time Xarchiver should be used.

Documentation: Built-in Help.

LXDE: Menu → Sound & Video → ISO Master
i3wm: iso – isomaster

Running on Removable Storage

Short of a PC itself failing, having bootable USB sticks and SD Cards insures a system will always be usable. MicroSD to USB adapters are inexpensive and small. As an example of a robust suite of chips:

1 USB Stick – Debian Live – 8GB
1 USB Stick – Work in Progress Backups – 64GB
3 USB Sticks – Backup Systems – 256GB
1 MicroSD Card – Primary System – 128GB
2 MicroSD Cards – Test Systems – 128GB

When working for long periods, save versions; MyFile1, MyFile2... At the end of a long work period do a Work in Progress Backup. Test Systems as well as the Primary System should be backed up. Then all it takes is a restore to reset a Test System. Backup a system at least once a month.

As a matter of security, physical access is total access. Removable storage can be placed in a safe or stay with the user when not in use. For shared machines, each user can have their own chip.

Keeping an already installed OS and running Linux on removable storage is an alternative to dual booting. Where Linux is the primary OS, running a second OS in a VM is another alternative to dual booting (Page 222).

Planning ahead, computers have a life span. Buying a new system every 3 to 4 years will avoid the panic of being without a system. It also provides a chance to break in a new system before it's needed. Older working systems can be used as backup systems.

Links

The Debian Website:
debian.org

More Distros:
kali.org
tails.net
distrowatch.com

More Software Sources:
snapcraft.io
flatpak.org
appimage.org
appimagehub.com
docker.com
store.steampowered.com
linuxlinks.com

Educational:
python.org
developers.google.com/machine-learning/crash-course
tensorflow.org
youtube.com search for: alphago the movie
ibm.com/z/resources/zxplore
linuxfromscratch.org
w3schools.com
geogebra.org

Go Paperless:
myboogieboard.com
getrocketbook.com

Hardware Recommendations

When looking for value be sure to check online eMalls, department stores, computer discount warehouses, and stores you frequent. End of Year Holiday and Beginning of School Year sales are good times to look for sales.

Single purpose adapters such as:
  USB-C to MicroSD Card $2 to $9.
Kingston, USB to SD and MicroSD Card Readers:
  About $10.
360 Electrical Surge Protector power strips:
  Outlets rotate helping with bulky transformers.
  Original versions did not have wall mounts,
  use L brackets and Velcro. About $19 to $40.
USB cords are cheaper to buy in bulk.
  Watch for fake painted braids.
  USB-C cords have 24 wires.
Logitech K400r keyboard:
  Long wireless reach, integrated mousepad.
  From $12 to $35.
Hisense 40" TV's as a second monitor.
  Look for 100$ to $150 sales.
  Turn on Graphic or Direct (Monitor) Mode.
Beelink, Mini PCs, high value, variety of models.
  Often requires a kernel update (Page 26),
  meaning newer technology.
Creality Ender 3, Open Source 3D Printer:
  About $200 .
NICGID, Sling Bag, variety of sizes and colors:
  About $25.

CLI BASH Reference

```
help                          | BASH help
man <command>                 | Manual help
env                           | Environment
history                       | Previous commands
whoami                        | Show user
touch <file>                  | Create file
cp <from> <to>                | Copy file
mv <from> <to>                | Move / rename file
rm <file>                     | Delete file
ls                            | List files
ls -la                        | All with details
cd <directory>                | Change Directories
cd ..                         | Up directory level
mkdir <directory>             | Make directory
pwd                           | Current directory
rm -r <directory>             | Delete directory
which <program>               | Show location
cat <file>                    | Read text file
cat > <file>                  | Write text file
cat >> <file>                 | Append Ctl+D
sudo chmod +x gol.sh          | Make executable
sudo pcmanfm                  | SU File Manager
passwd                        | Set User password
sudo passwd <id>              | Set <id> password
sudo usermod -aG <g> <id>     | Add User to Group
groups <id>                   | Show User groups
sudo dmesg                    | Display log
```

Using **Synaptic** install: debian-refcard   The files will install here: /usr/share/doc/debian-refcard/ gz files.

Open gz files with **Xarchiver** (Menu→ Accessories → **Xarchiver**), then open the pdf with **qpdfview**.

TROUBLESHOOTING

The trend of electronics is toward smaller, more durable, and lower cost. Maverick designs like the Asus Eee PC and the Raspberry Pi line of computers have driven innovation. Leading to designs like the Intel NUC, Next Unit of Computing and high value brands like Beelink. It's not how big the computer is, it's what you can do with it.

There are many forms of SSDs (Solid-State Drives). MicroSD cards and USB Flash drives are the most accessible. SSDs are digital and have a processor to manager the cells which make up the storage including spare cells. There have even been projects to install Linux on SSDs.

If a computer wont turn on, possibly swapping the power supply may resolve the issue. Generally it is not cost effective to repair computers. The goal will be to recover the SSD and the data on it, or destroy the SSD. Do you really want to hand a computer with everything your PC knows about you to anyone? This chapter will offer recommendations. Your system, your rules.

Troubleshooting

Protect your data and your time, backup your system. See Page 241.

- For forgotten passwords see Page 28.
- Stuck at LightDM login screen see Page 204.
- For disk (SSD) issues, boot from a Backup System.
  - From a terminal:
    - `sudo su`
    - `df -h`   (Find device & partition, example sdb2)
    - `umount /dev/sdb2`
    - `fsck.ext4 -p /dev/sdb2`
    - Reboot, if there issue persists:
      - `fsck.ext4 -fvy /dev/sdb2`
    - Generally the system is self recovering. If fsck recovery fails, it may be possible to reformat and restore the system from a backup. This may also be a sign the SSD should be replaced. There are more involved procedures that can be found on the internet.
- The system has internet, but is unable reach a website.
  - See Page 30, Network Fix.
- The system is unable to connect to an internet source.
  - From a terminal:
    - sudo rm -r /usr/lib/connman/*
    - It will be necessary to reselect networks and reenter passwords.
- System looses audio, see Page 189.
- Program fails to start.
  - Launch from a terminal.
  - Check apparmor Page 240.
  - Use strace Page 282.
- Synaptic issues see Page 284.

Rebuilding from Backups

Review the chapter on Backups, Page 241.

- Boot from a **Backup stick** with **persistence**.
  - Use **GParted** to format and setup partitions.
  - **Disable journaling** for any **ext4** partitions.
  - Restore the system from a backup.
- Alternatively do a fresh install.
  - Boot from a **Backup stick** without **persistence**.
  - Do a fresh install.
  - **Disable journaling** for any **ext4** partitions.
  - Boot from a **Backup stick** with **persistence**.
  - Restore the system from a backup.

Rebuilding with a new PC

Backup sticks are **Debian Live** chips and are not tuned to a specific system, they may be used to boot a **new system**, PC or Laptop. Do **NOT** install backups from one system onto another system.

- Boot the **new system** using a **Backup stick** without **persistence**, and do a fresh install on the new system.
- Review **Installing Debian** see Page 20.
- Then reboot the **new system** using the **Backup stick** with **persistence**. Restore the most current backup to a **temporary chip**.
- Reboot the **new system** without the **Backup stick**.
- Insert the **temporary chip** and copy over any required data files.

strace

Not all programs will work on all computers. There are times when searching the internet will provide no help, man files and logs files provide no clues, and even starting a program from LXTerminal provides no helpful messages. For source code see Page 156.

strace records system calls, **-o** sends the output to a text file, **-C** shows a summary. The file can be viewed with any text editor. **cat** can be a quick way to view a file. Piping the output to less, **| less**, allows the file to be scrolled using the Cursor Up / Down keys, Q to quit. cmatrix is used as an example, any program can be used.

From Synaptic install:
```
manpages-dev
strace
```

From LXTerminal:
```
man syscalls
Q
man strace
Q
strace --help
strace -C -o st.txt cmatrix
Q
cat st.txt | less
Q
```

The Linux **Programming Interface** by **Michael Kerrisk** – The definitive guide to the Linux / UNIX programming interface.

Your Linux Toolbox by **Julia Evans** - Presented as a series of handwritten stick figure comic books, the books provide exceptional tips for trouble shooting.

Memory Issues

Large programs such as Flowblade are more susceptible to issues such as memory leaks. Monitoring memory usage allows an opportunity to gracefully restart a program before a memory leak causes a system to crash. Memory can be monitored with **htop**, **free**, and the **Resources Monitors** plugin (Page 36). **stress-ng** can be used to stress test a system.

htop, top left:

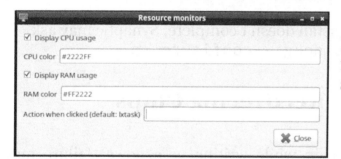

Resources monitors settings.

Memory shown in blue, CPU in red:

free has many options, **-s 10** runs every 10 sconds, **-c 20** runs 20 times, >> can send output to a file.
From a terminal:

```
free
free --help
free -s 10 -c 20
date >> memory.txt
echo >> "Testing procedure A"
free -s 10 -c 1000 >> memory.txt
```

Fixing Synaptic

If there are issues with Synaptic, try updating the package list. From time to time the package list should be update by clicking the **Reload** button on the toolbar, top left. If there have been major updates to the Debian repository, it may be necessary to do a **dist-upgrade**:

From a terminal:
```
sudo apt update -y
sudo dist-upgrade -y
```
Click the Synaptic **Reload** button, Toolbar top left.

If a package install doesn't complete, Synaptic may ask you to: `sudo dpkg --configure -a`

Recovering Chips

Removing a chip while writing or a power failure may panic a chip and make the chip read only, those chips may not be recoverable. GParted can generally format chips with ease. In a few cases there may be formatting or con-trol characters that are causing issues. Blindly write to the chip, overwriting the data on it will allow GParted to for-mat the chip. From a terminal, using **sdb** as an example:

```
sudo su
shred -v -n1 /dev/sdb
dd if=/dev/zero of=/dev/sdb bs=1024 count=1024
```

<u>Use care with **shred** and **dd**.</u> Shred can be used with files, partitions, and devices. See man shred and shred --help.

LINUX ON ANDROID

Linux can be run as an app on the Android platform without rooting. Projects which focus on Linux on Android without rooting include, Debian noroot by Pelya, UserLAnd by UserLAnd Technologies, and LINUXONANDROID by the GNU (linuxonandroid.com).

This section will focus on UserLAnd available thru the Google Play Store. UserLAnd currently uses a built-in VNC interface which does not allow audio or OpenGL graphics. However it is amazing what will run.

Many USB hubs, memory sticks, SD Card adapters and keyboards will work with Android. A USB-C to USB or Micro USB to USB adapter will often be required. There are also portable folding Bluetooth keyboards. Windows keyboards are more suited for use with Linux than Android keyboards. For small screen devices, screen casting, screen magnifiers, or magnifying glasses are helpful. Magnifying glasses are likely the most helpful.

Install Linux on Android

From the Play Store install **UserLAnd** (Does <u>not</u> require rooting). It is a good practice to make sure the Android device is fully charged before starting the install. For practical use a keyboard is required, a USB-C to USB or Micro USB to USB is all that is needed ($2 to $10, handy to have, cheaper in packs). For small screen devices magnifying glasses are required. A full install including a desktop will likely take about an hour. The Android device should be in landscape mode.

<u>The 3 Sections of UserLAnd:</u>
Section menu runs along the bottom of the screen.
1) **Apps: Install** Debian.
2) **Sessions: Start** and **Stop** Debian.
3) **Filesystems: Delete**, **Backup**, and **Restore**.

<u>Install Debian and LXDE:</u>
From the **Apps** section:
  Select **Debian**.
  Grant the permissions requested by UserLAnd.
  Please select a desktop environment:
    Select **Minimal** and click **CONTINUE**.
  Please select a connection type:
    Select **Graphical** and click **CONTINUE**.
  After install completes a **Linux Terminal** will open.
  Use the Android 2 finger pinch to zoom.

Install **LXDE** from the Linux Terminal:
```
sudo apt update -y
sudo apt dist-upgrade -y
sudo apt install dialog -y
sudo apt install task-lxde-desktop -y
```

Configuring keyboard-configuration panel:

Use the cursor Up / Down keys to select a keyboard.
Tab moves between OK and Cancel.
OK should be selected.
Press the Spacebar or Enter to continue.

```
sudo apt install x11-xserver-utils -y
sudo apt install dbus-x11 -y
sudo apt install openbox-lxde-session -y
sudo apt install wm-icons -y
sudo apt install gdu -y
sudo apt install nano -y
```

Create an LXDE Start Up script:

```
cd /usr/bin
nano go1
  openbox-lxde &> /dev/null &
  sleep 5
  dbus-launch pcmanfm --desktop &> dev/null &
  lxpanel &> /dev/null &
```
Ctrl + O, Enter, to save. Ctrl + X to exit.
```
chmod +x go1
```

Create a script to run Synaptic:
If Android has
internet and Linux
doesn't, use the
Google DNS
(Page 30).

```
cd /usr/bin
nano gosyn
  xhost + &&
  sudo synaptic &&
  xhost -
```
Ctrl +O, Enter, to save. Ctrl + X to exit.
```
chmod +x gosyn
```
Change the Synaptic Menu **Command:** to **gosyn**.

Create these folders in the home directory:

Documents, Downloads, Music, PDF, Pictures, Videos, and Templates.

Start LXDE:
```
gol
```
The screen will look very confused, close UserLAnd.

Start UserLAnd:
From the UserLAnd **Menu**, top right, select **Settings**:
Select **Default Landing Page**, select **Sessions.**
Click on **Sessions** at the bottom of the screen.
Long click **Debian**, if running, select **Stop Session**.
Click on **Debian**, to start Debian.

From the Terminal start LXDE:
```
gol
exit
```

The **VNC floating menu** will appear over the desktop.
The left most icon allows the VNC menu to be moved.
From the VNC menu's menu (right most icon):
If using a keyboard, select **Disable Extra Keys**.

Note: If Android is blocking access to CPU usage, right click on the **CPU monitor**, bottom right, and select **Remove "Usage Monitor" from Panel**.

Set Time Zone:
Menu → System Tools → LXTerminal
```
sudo dpkg-reconfigure tzdata
```
Follow the instructions, then restart Debian.

To Exit:
Close any running programs.
From the **VNC menu's menu** select **Disconnect**.
Long click **Debian**, select **Stop Session**.
Close UserLAnd, Win + Enter will close UserLAnd.

UserLAnd File Locations:
Menu → System Tools → File Manager PCManFM:
  /storage/internal   For Tech.ula full
  /storage/sdcard   path is required.
  /host-rootfs/storage/**426B-9A39**
  /host-rootfs/storage/**426B-9A39**/Android/data/Tech.ula
External Computer:
  /Device 1/Android/data/tech.ula/files/storage
  /Device 2/Android/data/tech.ual/files/storage
From an Android Terminal, find SD Card, USB Stick id's:
  `gdu -d | grep media` -OR- `gdu -d | grep vold`
  Sample id output: ... /mnt/media_rw/**426B-9A39**

Synaptic:
  Searching by **Description and Name**, will run slow.
  Searching by **Name** or **Dependencies** will run fast.
  Most install warning / error messages can be ignored.

Desktop Icon Size:
  Changing the zoom level in PCMamFM will change
  the size of the Desktop Icons. From PCManFM:
  View → Zoom In / Out.

Appearance and Theme:
Desktop, right click, Appearance tab, Wallpaper:
  /usr/share/wallpapers/Debian Theme/contents/images
Menu → Preferences → Customize Look and Feel
  Icon Theme tab, GNOME-Brave
Menu Icon, right click, Menu Settings/
  /usr/share/icons/Vendor/scalable/emblems

Screen Resolution:
In /support/startVNCServerStep2.sh comment out, #:
  # echo $vncrc_line > /home/$INITIAL_USERNAME/.vncrc
To set the resolution, edit ~/.vncrc

ScummVM games Example:

Look in the directory, /usr/share/scummvm Use the **folder name** followed by the **name** inside the folder. Below, "**scummvm... ...sky &&**" should be on one line. From Synaptic install: beneath-a-steel-sky

From a terminal:

```
cd /usr/bin
nano gosky
  pulseaudio --start &
  sleep 2
  scummvm -f -p /usr/share/scummvm/
      beneath-a-steel-sky sky &&
  pulseaudio -k
```
Ctrl +O, Enter, to save. Ctrl + X to exit.
```
chmod +x gosky
```

Press F5 for game controls, hover over buttons to see their function. Click on **Text and Speech** to select **Text only**.

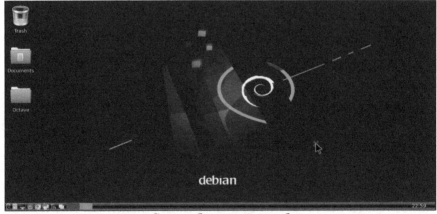

Configured LXDE Desktop

LINUX ON CHROMEBOOKS

The following section is included for those with Linux enabled Chromebooks. For Linux enabled Chromeboks, Linux is not an add-on, it's built-in. Linux can be installed with a click and removed with a click.

Install Linux

Chromebooks install Linux in a Container, inside a Virtual Machine, under Chrome OS. A Crosh session runs outside the Container. A Terminal session runs inside a Container. A Terminal session can manually be started from a Crosh session. To Install Linux the Chromebook must be connected to the internet. Navigate to the Linux development environment in Settings. Type **linux** in the **Settings Search Bar** and press Enter. Or, in Settings: About → Developers → Linux development environment.

Set Up Linux

Click the **Set up** button.

From the **Linux development environment** panel, click the **Set up** button.

Click the **Next** button.

The **Set up Linux development environment** panel will open, click the **Next** button.

Make Selections

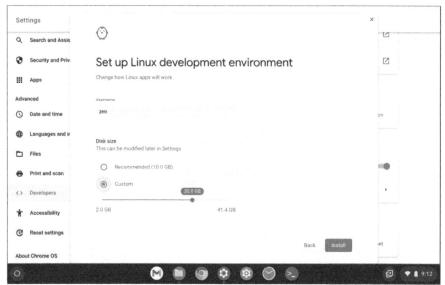

Click the **Install** button to continue.

Enter a **Username** and select the **Disk size** to be allocated to Linux. The **Username** can be any name. The **Disk size** can be changed at any time.

Removing Linux

Once the install is complete, Linux can be removed at anytime. From the **Linux development environment** panel, **Remove Linux development environment** section, click the **Remove** button.

Completing the Install

Installation should complete within minutes.

An **Installing Linux** panel will show the progress of the install.

Once the installation has completed, the **Terminal App** will open. A command prompt will be displayed:
<user-id>@penguin:$

It's handy to have the **Terminal App** pinned to the Taskbar. Right click on the Terminal icon and select Pin. Open the Terminal icon menu again and select Settings or Ctrl + Shift + P. Here the appearance of the Terminal app can be changed.

```
zen@penguin:~$ uname -a
Linux penguin 6.1.60-08594-g03a802b9a072 #1 SMP PREEMPT Wed Jan 24 19:12:12 PST 2024
aarch64 GNU/Linux
zen@penguin:~$ hostnamectl;
 Static hostname: penguin
       Icon name: computer-container
         Chassis: container ☐
      Machine ID: eba48fa4494b4c4a9d4630603c2ed5db
         Boot ID: b397a90f85704f9292efbcb49e709f22
  Virtualization: lxc
Operating System: Debian GNU/Linux 12 (bookworm)
          Kernel: Linux 6.1.60-08594-g03a802b9a072
    Architecture: arm64
zen@penguin:~$ cat /etc/os-release
PRETTY_NAME="Debian GNU/Linux 12 (bookworm)"
NAME="Debian GNU/Linux"
VERSION_ID="12"
VERSION="12 (bookworm)"
VERSION_CODENAME=bookworm
ID=debian
HOME_URL="https://www.debian.org/"
SUPPORT_URL="https://www.debian.org/support"
```

Once installation completes Terminal opens.

Enter the following five commands to learn more about the system:

```
uname -a
hostnamectl;
cat /etc/os-release
cat /etc/debian_version
getconf LONG_BIT
```

From this it can be seen the Google container name is Penguin. The actual Distro is Debian 12 Bookworm. The architecture is also important, will likely be AMD / Intel or ARM. getconf LONG_BIT will show whether the system is running as a 32 or 64 bit system.

Now set the user and root passwords. The command for password has a unique spelling, passwd. The password will need to be entered twice for each id.

```
sudo passwd <user-id>
sudo passwd root
```

LXDE on Chromebooks

LXDE on a Chromebook.

Install the LXDE Desktop, the nano editor, and nested X server Xephyr. LXDE will provide the desktop environment. Xephyr keeps the desktop intact. The lightdm greeter is not used by the ChromeOS container system and is disabled to prevent it from causing issues. From the Terminal App:

```
sudo apt update -y
sudo apt dist-upgrade -y
sudo apt install task-lxde-desktop -y
sudo apt install xserver-xephyr -
sudo apt install nano -y
sudo systemctl disable lightdm
```

LXDE Launch Script

```
 GNU nano 5.4                    gol *
Xephyr -br -fullscreen -resizeable :20 &
sleep 5
DISPLAY=:20 startlxde &
█



















^G Help      ^O Write Out^W Where Is ^K Cut     ^T Execute
^X Exit      ^R Read File^\ Replace  ^U Paste   ^J Justify
```

Nano: ^ is short for Ctrl key.

Using Nano create the file gol. Resizable is spelled wrong.
From the Terminal App:

```
sudo nano /usr/bin/gol
   Xephyr -br -fullscreen -resizeable :20 &
   sleep 5
   DISPLAY=:20 startlxde &
```
When done, Ctrl + O , Enter to save. Ctrl + X exit.

```
sudo chmod +x /usr/bin/gol
```

```
gol
```

LXDE Startup and Shutdown

Startup:
    Run the **Terminal** App.
    Select **Penguin** from the Terminal menu.
    gol
    Press Fullscreen if needed.

Shutdown (LXDE shuts down with Terminal):
    Exit any running Linux programs.
    Right click on the **Terminal** icon
    and select **Shut down Linux**.

Note: When Starting Linux after a Chromebook update the Chromebook should be connected to the internet. If Linux is also updated the start up will take longer than normal.

Crosh and Terminal

Everything on a Chromebook can be run through the Chrome browser. Crosh runs outside a Linux Container. Terminal runs inside a Linux Container. To be clear, Termina is a virtual machine, Terminal is a Terminal interface. Three important Chrome URL's to bookmark:

    chrome-untrusted://crosh
    chrome-untrusted://terminal
    chrome://about

Navigating from Crosh to Terminal

Navigating from Crosh, outside a container, to the inside of a container is a short process. Allow one command to finish before entering the next command. Enter the URL **chrome-untrusted://crosh** in the Chrome Browser. Ctrl + Shift + P opens preferences. Enter the following commands, **\<user-id\>** is your user id:

```
vmc start termina
lxc start penguin
lxc exec penguin su - <user-id>
gol
```

LXDE will start, return to the Chrome Browser. If LXDE is covering the Chrome Browser, just press Fullscreen. Enter the following commands:

```
exit
lxc stop penguin
exit
vmc stop termina
```

If termina is misspelled while starting termina (vmc start termina), a new virtual machine will be started with the new name. To correct this, exit the VM, stop it, then destroy it. Any containers inside it will also be deleted:

```
vmc start pug
exit
vmc list
vmc stop pug
vmc destroy pug
```

When Terminal won't Start

If Terminal wont start, reboot the Chromebook and place the Chromebook online then restart Linux. If that fails try the following:

1) First try:
   From the Chrome OS Chrome Browser:
   From the Crosh URL:
   chrome-untrusted://crosh
   ```
   vmc stop termina
   ```

2) If that fails then:
   From the Chrome OS Chrome Browser
   From the URL:
   chrome-untrusted://crosh
   ```
   vmc start termina
   lxc stop penguin
   exit
   vmc stop termina
   ```

3) If that fails, last try :
   From **Terminal**
   Select **Penguin** from the Terminal menu.
   ```
   sudo halt
   ```
   Restart **Terminal** and select **Penguin**, then do:
   Ctrl + C
   From the Chrome OS Chrome Browser:
   From the Crosh URL:
   chrome-untrusted://crosh
   ```
   vmc stop termina
   ```

4) Reboot the Chromebook, start at step one.

Sommelier – Wayland Compositor

Description: Sommelier is a Wayland compositor, it handles session connections to Linux. There is no one size fits all solution for every program. Sommelier can be run as a wrapper around a program, allowing custom settings for that program. Scale will vary.

Documentation: sommelier --help

Three recommended Prefix options:
1) No prefix.
2) env GDK_BACKEND=x11 <program-name>
3) sommelier -X --scale=.5 --glamor
   --frame-color=#000000 <program-name>

Lower case **sommelier**, space, dash, capital **X**, space, dash, dash, lower case **scale**, equal, point 5, space, dash, dash, lower case **glamor**, space, dash, dash, lower case **frame**, dash, **color**, equal, pounds sign, six zeros, space, program name. When sommelier is used as a prefix, the program will run outside the desktop while appearing to run on the Desktop. Clicking on the Desktop will cause the program to disappear, press Show windows and select the program to restore it.

Scale will vary with the Chromebook Display settings, screen size, and the program. A good staring point for high resolution is a scale .5, a good starting point for low resolution is a scale of 1.2. The larger the number, the smaller the screen. The smaller the number, the larger the screen. If .3 is a little too large and .4 is a little too small, try .35. Try the Fullscreen key, sometimes it works.

To edit an LXDE menu item, right click on it, select **Properties**, **Desktop Entry** tab, edit the **Command:**, this will also fix i3wm. ~/.local/share/applications/ <name>.desktop are override files and can be manually edited or deleted without hurting anything.

When a menu item is edited, it is copied from:
   /usr/share/applications
To:
   ~/.local/share/applications/

Check a program's documentation for command line options. Also check a program's settings. If a program is glitchy, try lowering it's resolution and possibly turn off features. Most programs will have a fullscreen option in their settings.

To keep the Chrome OS Taskbar hidden while using Linux, right click on the Chrome OS Taskbar and select **Autohide shelf**. Press Show windows right click on the Taskbar and select **Always show shelf** from the menu to restore.

Keeping Apps on the Desktop

Some Linux programs like LXTerminal require a change to their launch command to keep them on the desktop. It may be necessary to restart Linux for the change to take effect. Change the LXTerminal launch command.

From:
   lxterminal
To:
   env GDK_BACKEND=x11 lxterminal

Index A - K

Index L - S

Index T - W

T

Terminal:
  LXTerminal – 44
  XTerm – 50-51, 214
Tiddly Wiki - 173-184
Tiling Window Manager – see
  i3wm
Troubleshooting – 279
TWM – 212

U

UEFI – 28, 221-236
Unicode – 270
USB Sticks – See Chips
Users and Groups:
  Managing – 265

V

VM:
  Aqemu – 222-233, 260
  OVMF – 233
  QEMU – 232-233
  VMM – 234
VS Code – 170-171

W

Web Server:
  Apache – 219
  Printer – 198
WiFi – see Internet/Connman

Just for Fun

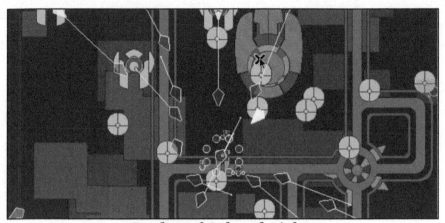

Garden of Colored Lights
For Fullscreen, edit ~/.garden/init.txt and
set Windowed = 0 (zero).

In over 20 years of watching Linux, there's always more to learn and more to explore. A visit to distrowatch.com can provide an idea of how many Linux distros there are. Linux runs on everything from cell phones to mainframes. 3D printers are available starting in the $200 range. Paper models can be printed on a standard printer.

Googling printable paper models will produce endless pages of results. Construction usually requires a color printer, scissors, cardstock and glue. PosteRazor (Page 80) can be used to enlarge images. LibreOffice Draw and Gimp (Page 78) can be used to create and edit images. Business card magnets can be used to tile posters and other objects to make them magnetic. Some printed materials can be painted with polyurethane or other like materials to make them more durable.

ABOUT THE AUTHOR

R.S. Ake started programming back in the days of the S-100 microcomputers and never stopped. He is very grateful to have worked in the field of IT his entire life. He has known exhaustion, but never boredom. He is a fan and long time user of Linux. He is inspired by curiosities like the game of life running inside the game of life, the most beautiful equation in math, and the logic machine of Lewis Carroll.

Also Available

The Chromebook Guide to Google Linux
2nd Edition (Blue Cover)

Installing Linux On PCs and Laptops

Companion Videos

By Ruth Ake (Daughter of R.S. Ake) available on YouTube
youtube.com/@ruthake

Made in the USA
Monee, IL
23 October 2024

68511503R00174